MAKING THE MOST OF A
MESSY MARRIAGE

JAY AND LAURA LAFFOON

WITH BROOKE CHAVEZ

ILLUSTRATED BY GORDON WHITNEY

Welcome

I (Laura) know a few things. I know I am a mess. I know my husband is a mess. I also know you are a mess. We are all a mess! Not one of us is getting through this thing called life unscathed. If you're honest with yourself, you know it's true.

That's probably why you picked up this book. Congratulations! If you are looking for help for your messy marriage, you have come to the right place. We have learned a few things along the way through our 35-year-long, very messy marriage. We know from experience that messy doesn't have to mean hopeless.

Get ready to learn. Get ready to be challenged. Get ready to work hard, serve your spouse, practice selflessness and self-sacrifice, and get ready to have an amazing marriage that defies the odds. We believe what God has in store for your marriage will blow your mind. So go ahead, admit to yourself that you are a mess, and lets get on with making the most of this messy thing we call marriage.

Blessings,

Jay & Laura

Table of Contents

Part One

Chapter 1

How Our Mess Began

"The book of love has music in it.
In fact, that's where music comes from..."
Peter Gabriel

Webster's Dictionary defines a "mess" as *a dirty, untidy, or disordered condition; a person or thing that is dirty, untidy, or disordered; a state of embarrassing confusion.*

Disordered? Untidy? A state of embarrassing confusion? That sounds about right.

Based on these definitions, I think we can all agree in some way, shape, or form, we are all a mess. Messy people who have come together in marriage are naturally going to have a messy marriage. That's certainly true for us. We are no exception. The proof of our messy marriage is in the pudding! We'd like to tell you the story of how it all got started.

Three Rules of Dating

On July 3, 1984, I (Jay) moved from my hometown of Petoskey,

Michigan, to Atlanta, Georgia, to begin a job I secured after graduating from college. Exactly one day later, I was set up on a blind date with Laura Elizabeth Bass.

My friends and I arrived at Laura's house thirty minutes early. At this point I became keenly aware of the first rule dating:

1. Don't show up half an hour early!

I knocked on the door for what seemed like an eternity. After each knock, I would turn to Chaz and Deaver—the couple who set this date up—and stare with disbelief. *Is this girl standing me up before we've even met?* My self-esteem was withering by the millisecond.

We were just about to leave when the door swung open. The next moment is a bit of a blur. I remember being surprised to see a young woman who had obviously just gotten out of the shower. Her hair was soaking wet and strung all over her face. She stood in front of us in nothing but a T-shirt and boxer shorts, clutching a towel to her chest in an obvious attempt at modesty. I stuck out my hand.

"Hi, I'm Jay," I said, with every bit of personality I could muster.

Laura let out an embarrassed, Jr. High giggle and promptly turned toward Deaver with a look that sent chills down my spine. Now that I think about it, that look has been aimed at me a time or two—or a thousand—since then. Chaz and I went into the living room and turned on TBS; I think we were watching *The Andy Griffith Show*. Deaver went with Laura while she got ready. Twenty minutes later I learned the second rule of dating:

2. When women go away together, miracles happen.

I looked up and saw beauty. The shower-soaked woman I met at the door had been transformed. I was dumbfounded.

The four of us went to an Atlanta Braves game. I remember it vividly. I remember I paid too much for the tickets. I remember the food was awful. I also remember that Laura and I talked about *everything*. I had spent time with many members of the opposite sex before. In fact, some of my best friends were women. This was different. The conversation flowed like a mighty river—deep and strong. I was amazed by the intensity so early in the relationship.

When the game ended, the lights in the stadium went dark, and July 4th fireworks lit up the sky, eliciting oooo's and aaaaah's from the crowd. Afterward, Chaz grabbed Deaver's hand and bolted for the gate to beat the crowd. Deaver instinctively grabbed Laura's hand, and in turn Laura grabbed mine.

My heart leaped out of my chest.

It was strange. I've held many girls' hands before, but this made my entire body feel like it was going into a seizure. My arms, legs, and head reeled in every direction because of the ecstasy. It scared me to death.

I barely spoke on the way home, quietly analyzing the situation. That may be why Laura got out of the car so quickly. She left without so much as a goodnight handshake. Still, I must have made an impression. The next morning, when Laura's mom asked her how the date went, she replied without hesitation, "Mom, I'm going to marry that man!"

Over the next ten days, I learned the third and final rule of dating:

3. If a woman wants to marry you, give up!

They should teach a course for men in every college across America called Give Up 101. It would save us all a tremendous amount of pain and suffering. In a city of two million people, Laura managed to have our paths cross eight of the next ten days. To this day I don't know how she did it. We have a word for this now. It's called stalking!

The coup d'etat took place when she asked me—and I agreed—to a weekend trip to the mountains with her and her friends. That Saturday night, ten days after our blind date, in a log cabin on a mountain in North Carolina, I asked Laura Elizabeth Bass to be my wife. Her reply?

"What took you so long?"

The Ring

Three hundred dollars was all the money I had in the world. After I moved to Atlanta and paid my first month's rent, I had three hundred bucks left over. I told Laura I couldn't afford a ring yet, and she assured me it was okay.

I appreciated her graciousness, but I wanted to give her a ring. To me, a ring was a symbol of my love and commitment to her. I couldn't wait for the moment when I could slide that symbol on her finger. That moment, it turned out, was not far off.

The day after I asked Laura to be my wife was a day from heaven: Carolina blue sky, billowing clouds, and my new fiancée sitting right beside me as we drove back to Atlanta. I lay in bed that night with my heart on fire. I was in love, and nothing else in the world mattered. That is, until Monday morning.

4

As soon as I got to work, I knew something had changed. I had been there only a week or so, but I could tell something big was going down. The company I had come to Atlanta to work for—the reason I moved a thousand miles from home—was closing its doors. I was out of work.

My life turned upside down and inside out. I was in love, but I had no job, no money, and no place to live. As Dickens so aptly put it, "It was the best of times; it was the worst of times." What would I tell Laura? What would I tell my parents?

Laura was gracious once again. "First," she said with a smile, "I have money; second, you can live with my mom if you need to; and the ring . . . well, I'll get it when I get it. Now kiss me!"

What a woman! At that moment I knew why I had moved to Atlanta. I knew why I was here. It was to begin the rest of my life with the woman my mom had been praying for since I was young. I truly felt peace in the midst of the storm.

When I rang the house, Mom spoke first before I could relay my news. "I'm so glad you called. I've got some business to cover with you."

She proceeded to tell me of a life insurance policy she and Dad had taken out for me years before. She told me I could keep it or cash it in. Cash! I didn't know why we hadn't covered this bit of "business" before I left home, but the thought of $2,000.00 in my palms was just what I needed. It was time to tell them my news.

"Mom," I said, "put Dad on the other phone. I've got some good news and some bad news." I then told them about Laura.

"JAY WILLIAM LAFFOON, YOU DO NOT TELL YOUR MOTHER YOU'RE ENGAGED OVER THE PHONE AFTER KNOWING THIS GIRL ONLY TEN DAYS! I certainly hope this is the bad news."

I winced. "Well, Mom, actually that was the good news." Silence. Dead air. Nothing.

"We trust you, Son. Go on." Dad's voice. It was like a bell ringing on the steeple of a church, comforting and encouraging. I also told them about my job. As we talked, we began to revel in the fact that the insurance issue was just now coming up. God's timing is perfect!

If I had wanted, I could have scraped by on $2,000.00 for quite some time, but I was a man on a mission. That money was my ticket to an engagement ring, and nothing would stand in my way.

After days of shopping I purchased the ring and devised a plan to give it to Laura. I would surprise her with it on top of a beautiful mountain. This mountain was located in a camp that my dad directed every summer near Woodland Park, Colorado. Soldier's Mountain lies on the backside of the range that runs beside the U.S. Air Force Academy. At the peak is a cross made from pine trees, wedged between two large rocks.

The view from the top of Soldier's Mountain is nothing short of spectacular: a postcard picture of Pike's Peak and the surrounding mountain ranges. I would give Laura the ring on top of Soldier's Mountain, at the foot of the cross.

To put it mildly, I was excited. We drove from Atlanta to Colorado Springs with very few stops. We slept an hour in a rest area in western Kansas until the sunrise woke us, and we were on our way again. I had hidden the ring and a bottle of cham-

6

pagne, compliments of the diamond store, in Laura's backpack. My idea was to order two pan pizzas from Pizza Hut in Woodland Park and hike to the top of Soldier's Mountain. After we had enjoyed our pizza and bubbly, I'd give her the ring.

The hike up Soldier's takes about twenty minutes, depending on your physical condition and the number of times you stop to take picture after picture of this place touched by the hand of God. I kept pushing us to get to the top.

"You've got to see it, you've just got to see it," I kept saying.

Laura reminded me we had just driven twenty-four hours straight, gotten little sleep, and were now operating at 8,500 feet above sea level.

About halfway up, I saw something moving down the trail toward us at a rapid speed. We stepped to the side. Being in the middle of Pike's Peak National Forest, a bear or mountain lion was not at all out of the question, and neither would make for good company. But the view cleared, and bounding down the trail came a twelve-year-old boy. He was running so fast he was nearly out of control.

From fifty feet away he yelled, "ARE YOU JAY LAFFOON?"

"Yes!" I hollered back, and by the time I answered, he was twenty feet past me.

"GOOOOOOD!" he bellowed, not even breaking stride.

My best friend in the world was Dean Moyer, a college bud who moved to Atlanta to work for the same company I did. He phoned ahead and arranged for a single red rose and a card to be delivered to the foot of the cross on the top of the mountain. Laura got to the cross first and saw the rose.

"Hey, there's a flower," she said with her sweet southern drawl.

"Have a look," I said.

"Oh, it has a card."

"Interesting. What does it say?"

She read the message aloud. "Congratulations, Jay and Laura. Love, Dean." She looked confused. "What do you suppose that means?"

My plan was unraveling before my eyes, so I had to think quickly. "Oh, Dean's always doing things like this. He's just congratulating us on climbing the mountain. Awfully nice of him." I waited for her reply, hoping she bought my story.

"Oh, isn't that sweet? How nice."

Phew! It went right over her head. At that moment I was very, very thankful Laura had been a cheerleader in college.

The pizza was now cold and the champagne very warm. We had just gotten out of our car and climbed over a thousand feet to the top of the mountain. We sat with our legs dangling over the edge of the cliff with the cross right above us. We looked out over the marvelous landscape that was being drenched by the noontime sun. The moment had arrived.

I reached in the backpack and pulled out the jewelry box. I opened it and held my hands toward Laura.

"Honey, I know I've asked you this, and I know you said yes, but I want to make it official. Will you marry me?"

At that moment her bottom lip began to quiver. It was cute at first, but I now know what that quiver means. Sweat began to bead up on her forehead. I'd never seen Laura sweat before. I now know what that sweat means. The look on her face was puzzling, like it was caught halfway between extreme joy and agony. I now know what that look means.

Nothing came out of her mouth for what seemed like an eternity. Nervously, I asked again.

"Honey? Will you marry me?"

At that moment the word yes did not come out of her mouth. Neither did the word no. But something did come out of her mouth. This woman I loved, this woman I was asking to marry me, this woman I wanted to spend the rest of my life with, spewed an uninterrupted stream of pizza, champagne, and gastrointestinal juices my direction. Laura puked her guts all over me! She could have sent it over the edge of the cliff; she could have turned her head the other way, but no, she had to barf all over me.

Does this mean yes?

Immediately she began to laugh. At first I failed to find the humor, but slowly a smile crept over my face as she put the ring on her finger and hugged me, all covered with goop.

"Yes, yes, yes, yes, yes!" she said, laughing. "Don't you know that in the South, a woman must puke on a man before she can marry him?"

We wiped the remains off the corners of her mouth and off the front of me. I will never forget that day. Or that smell!

We started this marriage a mess and the mess continues.

Another Messy Love Story

My name is Brooke. I'm a wife to a great guy and a mom of a sweet, but strong-willed little girl. I'm also a part-time farmer, a writer, and a nature enthusiast. I am most passionate about marriage and family. You'll be hearing from me here and there throughout this book. To start off, I'm going to tell you the story of another messy marriage... mine!

I grew up like many young women in Christian circles who were told to envision their perfect man and make their list so that they wouldn't settle for any old guy who came along. I was among the generation of Christian girls waiting for "the one". Ha! I found him alright.

I found *the one* who would drive me crazy. *The one* who would be my best friend and sometimes, my nemesis. *The one* who would rub me the wrong way. *The one* who would irk all of my last nerves. *The one* who would push me to the end of myself so that I had to rely on God to make this thing work. He is "the one" alright.

I met Pablo when I was a Senior in high school. I played guitar in a church worship band, and I got asked to travel with a worship team from a ministry training program called Master's Commission. The group was bilingual. There were both English and Spanish-speaking students.

Pablo was one of those spanish-speaking students. He had come over from Mexico to study with Master's Commission.

10

He was tall and dark and handsome, although I didn't like his style at first. He was too straight-laced for me. I had short, spiky hair, and wore a studded belt and wide-leg jeans. He slicked his hair straight back in classic mexican style and tucked in his T-shirts. Ew. Nerd alert!

Oh, and I forgot to mention, Pablo didn't speak a lick of English. Needless to say, there wasn't a lot in the form of chemistry between us.

Fast-forward a year. I graduated high school and entered Master's Commission myself. I was studying the Bible and growing in my faith, my musical abilities were being stretched and challenged, and I was becoming very interested in learning this spanish I'm hearing spoken all around me. In fact, I have just spent a year doing ministry in a spanish-language church, ministering in spanish-speaking communities, singing spanish songs, and falling in love with Hispanic culture. Meanwhile, Pablo has been living in the States for a while, he's relaxed his style a little, and he's learned a little English. The stage has been set.

Somewhere near the end of that year in Master's Commission, Pablo was promoted to worship leader of the spanish-language church we had been serving in, and he asked me to play guitar in his band. At that first practice, when I heard Pablo sing for the very first time, the heavens opened. An aura of golden light shone down on his handsome brown head, and it seemed as if he were singing just to me. His eyes closed and opened in slow motion as his perfect lips formed each heavenly word. I was in love. From that point on it was my mission to let him know that I was interested.

It didn't take long for him to get the hint. By the time graduation came, we both had stars in our eyes.

We spent the summer apart. Pablo was in Mexico renewing his visa to come back to the States, and I was pining over him. We officially started dating a couple weeks after he returned. I don't know... something like Sunday, September 24th, 2006 at around 7pm, on a swing in the backyard of our dormitory. That beautiful, warm evening began a long journey of learning that we are still on; learning to communicate, learning to make sacrifices, learning to choose each other. Pablo has been the one who has taught me the most about myself, about life, and about God.

Remember that list I had? Yeah. Crumple that up and toss it away. Pablo fulfilled only one requirement on that list: an accent. I'd always dreamed I'd marry a man with an accent and I'd listen to him read to me for the rest of my life. Of course, back then I imagined he'd have a Scottish or a British accent, but I'll take Pablo's Latin lilt over Billy Boyd's any day! (The first Lord of the Rings movie came out when I was in high school. I *might* have had a crush on one or more of the hobbits.)

I'll never forget my best friend's word of advice when I was still anguishing over whether or not Pablo could be "the one" God had for me.

She said, "Honey, if God meant for you to find one person he created for you, he wouldn't have given you 7 billion people to choose from. At some point, you have to decide if you can live with him or not."

You may or may not agree with my friend's statement. I sure didn't in that moment, but it was the first time I considered that maybe God had given me a choice in the matter.

Well, I did choose Pablo, and thankfully, he chose me too. We married four and a half years later on a cold, rainy day in April.

We are still choosing each other today, even after 8 wonderful years of marriage.

The Messy Bible People

One would think that if there was one place you could find people who had it all together, it would be the Bible. Unfortunately, you would have to keep looking. The Bible is a hall of fame for people who, despite being given every opportunity to succeed, royally screwed things up.

Let's start with Abraham and Sarah. Many of us would consider Abraham as the Father of our faith. He was the beginning of a covenant relationship with God, after Adam and Eve—we won't even talk about what a mess *they* were!

Abraham and Sarah were husband and wife. In Genesis 12, we find them traveling to Egypt. Abraham tells Sarah to pretend that they are brother and sister while they are in Egypt. That way, Abraham would be treated well by the Egyptians. That's messed up! When Pharaoh met Sarah, he thought she was single and ready to mingle. So, he took her to be his wife, which caused all kinds of problems. What a mess!

In the 29th chapter of Genesis, we read the story of Jacob, Leah and Rachel. Jacob was sent to his uncle after stealing the birthright from his brother. He met Rachel, fell in love and agreed to work for his uncle for 7 years in order to be given Rachel in marriage. At the end of those 7 years, his uncle snuck the other sister into the marriage tent. Jacob ended up marrying Leah instead of Rachel! But he was still in love with Rachel, so he agreed to work for another 7 years in order to marry Rachel, too. The story is a mess, but that fact the Jacob married two sisters? Messed up!

Moving on to David and Bathsheba. Their mess is found in 2 Samuel 11. David saw Bathsheba in the bath one night and just had to have her. He knew she was married, but he summoned her anyway and made love to her. Of course, she ended up pregnant.

David then tried to cover his tracks by bringing her husband, Uriah, home from war for a little "quality time" with his wife. Three different times he tried to make Uriah go home to Bathsheba so he would think the baby growing in her belly was his. Each time, Uriah refused out of loyalty to David and the troops still in the thick of battle.

Finally, David sent him back to the front lines of war so he will be killed. That's just some of David's drama, and this is the man whom the Bible refers to as "a man after God's own heart".

Even the parents of God himself, Joseph and Mary, were a mess. In the book of Luke, chapter 2, we read the story of Jesus being left in Jerusalem by his parents. I guess technically Jesus stayed behind on purpose, but his parents didn't realize he was missing for three days. Three days!

First, they thought he must be traveling with their relatives or friends. After not finding him there, they assumed he must still be in Jerusalem and went back. If this were a modern-day story, Jesus would have been placed in protective custody! It took them three days to even ask each other, "Hey, have you seen Jesus?"

"No, he's not with me. I thought he was with you."

Once they realized their mistake, they had to travel *three days* all the way back to Jerusalem to find him. That is a mess.

We are His Children

We are a mess and so are our kids. I (Laura) grew up in the south. I was taught manners growing up, and I expected the same from our children. We taught them from a young age to address adults with respect by saying "yes, sir," "no, sir," or "yes, ma'am" and "no ma'am".

When our daughter Grace was little, I wanted to make sure that she understood this concept, so I gave her a verbal quiz.

"What do you say to dad?" I asked her.

"No sir, yes sir," she replied.

Ok good. "What do you say to mom?"

"Yes ma'am, no ma'am."

Perfect. I then tried one we hadn't practiced before, just to see if she was really getting it.

"What do you say to grandma?" I asked.

She stopped and thought for a minute before she said, "Can I have a cookie...ma'am?"

Good girl. Quiz complete and she got a perfect score!

Our children are such a great example of how God relates to us. For some reason, we think we are supposed to have it all together. When our children make a mess, we get it. That's what children do. Even when they are older and make mistakes, we get it. That's how they learn. Why can't we extend that same grace to ourselves? We should, because we are

God's children. We make messes. It's what we do, and it is how we learn. God in heaven views us as his children. In fact, he *calls* us his children.

"See what love the Father has given us, that we should be called children of God! And that's what we are!" —1 John 3:1a

Despite the messes we make, we are God's children. He gets that. Imagine that your child just spilled his milk all over the floor. Instead of scolding him, you go to him. You reassure him that you still love him, that it was just an accident, and then you help him clean it up.

God has that same love for you. He is saying the same things over you. No matter how many times you screw it up, God is standing there with a towel saying, "Let's clean this up together. I still love you. You are my child and nothing you can do can make me love you less."

In marriage, there is bound to be some spilled milk. You are two different people who come from two different backgrounds. You are trying to mesh two different lives together. Whether you are winning or failing at that, your marriage is bound to be a bit messy. That is ok.

We're a mess. Our marriage is a mess. We have come to accept that and realize that it is not such a big deal, as long as our eyes are open to it. It takes recognizing our brokenness in our mental, emotional, sexual, and spiritual lives, and being ready to overcome it. In the next few chapters, we will look at each of these areas in more depth. We will also give you some steps you can take to make the most of your messy marriage.

Your Reflections

Take a few moments and write down some of the messiest parts of you marriage. I'm not talking about your sock drawer, though that may also need some attention! If you are reading this book with your spouse, share your answers with each other.

_____

_____

_____

_____

_____

_____

_____

_____

_____

_____

Chapter 2

We're all a MESS

Laura and I each have a healthy dose of our own individual mess. When we got married, we joined those messes in a commitment to each other. I don't know how it's working out for you, but for us, this has resulted in a messy marriage.

Early on we discovered a few differences that contribute to the mess. We both think very differently and process information differently. **Mentally we are a mess.**

Jay is up and down on the emotional roller coaster and I am more like a steady river. There's not a lot of changes in water level, just a little ebb and flow. **Emotionally we are a mess.**

I guess giving Jay a jar of green M&Ms after our blind date gave him the wrong impression about my sex drive. (Back in the day, it was said that green M&M's make you horny.) Jay on the other hand only wanted sex on days that end in the letter "Y". **Sexually we are a mess.**

The Bible tells us in Romans 3:23 that we have all sinned and fallen short of the glory of God. **Spiritually we are all a mess.**

Despite our mental, emotional, sexual and spiritual mess, we have found hope. Let's take a look at our messes in bite size pieces. By delving into what makes each of us a mess in any given area and then looking at what we can do about it, we can make our marriages a little less messy!

Frozen Fish

Let's start by tackling our mental mess. This one is a no brainer. Men and women take in information differently and process it differently. At the very core we think and value things differently. We're not even speaking the same language most of the time.

Just the other day, we were cooking dinner together. I (Laura) decided we would cook salmon. You've got to have your Omega 3's!

Normally, cooking together is something we enjoy doing, but this particular evening Jay was not being very enjoyable. I let a few minutes pass to see if he became more enjoyable before asking what his problem was.

"I hate frozen fish," he said.

Being the one who decided what we would cook for dinner, I took his response personally. "Why do you hate me?" I asked, becoming a little less enjoyable myself.

"Huh? I said I hate frozen fish, not you!"

"Yes but I picked out the fish, so you must hate me."

Yep, we are a mess.

Men and Women Think Differently

Isn't God hilarious? He made man. He made woman. He made them so different from one another. Then he said, "Wouldn't it be great if they married each other?" You could not unite two more different beings on the planet than a man and a woman. We are just so different!

Here's an example. When a man looks in the mirror, he sees everything he likes. He likes his nose. His new haircut is looking fresh. He's been working out and he can see a muscle right there. Oh, is that a bicep? Hello! Men pick out one or two things that are ok and focus on that.

When a woman looks in the mirror, however, she sees all the flaws. She hates her nose. Her hair is never quite like her stylist did it. She's been working out, but she is sure she has gained weight. Her shortcomings outweigh the positive and she focuses on them. We're different.

Recently, I (Laura) have been looking at other women's eyebrows. Why? I have no idea! I would speculate it is because I have a plethora of friends on social media who are doing live videos of applying makeup. One avenue of applying makeup is to add to and enhance the look of your brows.

I asked our daughter, Grace, who is a professional at skincare and makeup, for advice. She instructed me how to enhance my brows with a pencil and brush. When she did it for me they looked fabulous. I have yet to be able to replicate what she did. Every morning since then, I go to wash my face and end up obsessing over my brows. I have always been told what beautiful, thick eyebrows I have. Now I want them thinner so I can enhance them to look thicker myself. Oh, the irony! I should have just left them alone.

I'm just going to be honest right now. The mirror we are often looking into as women isn't the one in our bathrooms or over our vanities. Most of us are looking into the mirror of social media. The platforms you go to everyday are a great place to find where you don't measure up. Let's put down the mirror and be thankful. God made you good. You are good.

Back to the mess....

Now You May Speak

When Jay wakes up in the morning, he swings his feet out of the bed. The minute they hit the floor, his brain starts working. As soon as his brain starts working, his mouth starts talking. That is annoying for me. He is either awake or asleep, but no in between. There is no quiet, peaceful and somewhat groggy middle ground.

I, on the other hand, love my sleep. I hate getting out of bed in the morning. I need to warm up to the day. Don't talk to me before coffee. You won't like the response you'll receive. In fact, don't even talk at all! A few sips in, I MAY tolerate you, but i'm not really ready to have a conversation until I've drained the first cup.

Here's my perfect cup of coffee!

Brain Research Shows How Different We Are

It used to be generally accepted in the scientific world that men and women were the same at the brain level. Researchers attributed most observed differences in behavior and cognitive function between sexes as the learned influence of their predominant culture. New studies, however, are painting a different picture.

Diane Halpern, PhD and former president of the American Psychological Association, believed that mounting research indicated a biological difference between the male and female brain that influences typically male and typically female behaviors. While she agrees that culture plays a role in the development of our brains and our behaviors, she eventually published a text entitled *Sex Differences in Cognitive Abilities*, settling on the idea that men and women's brains are *biologically* different.

Neural circuitry mapping of over a 1000 brains revealed some unique differences in the way men's and women's brains are wired. It turns out that men's brained are highly connected between the front and back regions, and not as strongly across the right and left hemispheres. This allows the male a higher degree of coordination and perception. Women's brains, on the other hand, showed much higher connectivity between the hemispheres than from front to back. This allows for multitasking, and proficiency at tasks that require both intuitive and logical thinking. I think we've all known these differences for a while now. It's interesting to see that science backs it up!

Waffles and Spaghetti

Jay here. Our good friends Bill and Pam Farrel long ago noticed the differences in the way men and women think, and wrote a wonderful book entitled *Men are Like Waffles and Women are Like Spaghetti*. This serves as a great illustration for married couples to understand how your spouse's brain works.

For men, their brain is a lot like a waffle. It's filled with little boxes for each item, activity or thought to fit into. Only one thing fits in each little square. For example there may be a work box, a golfing box, and a box filled with love for his wife. There definitely is a sex box.

Women need to understand that a man can only be in one box at a time. For example, if he is in his golfing box about to go play 18 holes, he can't jump into a discussion about the kids and their after-school activities. That's another box entirely. You can talk about it, but he's not going to remember, because he's in his golfing box. This is incredibly frustrating to women. You've probably had this conversation with your husband:

"We talked about this!" she says, frustrated.

"No we didn't!" he replies, equally frustrated.

Ladies, your husband is not ignoring you. Don't assume he doesn't care. He DOES care about you and what you have to say. You just have to make sure he's in the right box at the right time. How do you make sure he's in the right box? That is easy. WAIT. That's right. Wait until he is not looking at a TV screen, a computer, or his phone. Wait until you have his full, undivided attention. Wait until he is looking at you in the eye. Then say, "I need to talk to you about _____." And wait for him to jump to that box. You are now ready to have a conversation that he will remember.

There are a few special boxes of which you ladies need to be aware:

- **The Hungry Box** -- Don't try to talk to him about ANY-THING if he's hungry. You will just make him hangry. (That's both hungry and angry. Not a fun combination!)

- **The Media Box** -- Don't try to talk to him if there is any form of media present—if the TV is on or he's in front of the computer or on his phone. To make sure he's in the box you want to discuss, wait until he is looking you in the eye. Any form of media will distract him and cause him to jump boxes.

- **The Sex Box** -- Don't even hint about going into the sex box unless you mean it. Why? He will jump into that box and stay in that box until you've had sex. If something happens and you are no longer in the mood, you will send him into the frustrated box, the angry box, or the pouting box. For most men, the sex box is very important.

- **The Jerk Box** -- Sometimes it feels like you've married a jerk. Chances are some of you have. When we're in our jerk box, 99% of the time it's not because of you. However, we know that 100% of the time you will feel like *you've* done something wrong. Simply ask if everything is OK. Remember most men don't want to be jerks, but they are lost in something going on outside your relationship. It could be as simple as his favorite team losing a game, or something deep like a rumor of layoffs at work. If you're not sure what's on his mind, ask.

- **The Nothing Box** -- We know this one drives you nuts. When you ask your husband what he's thinking and he says "nothing," don't try to analyze what he might be thinking about. He's literally thinking about *nothing*.

We all have a box we can go to and think about nothing. I call it my "happy place".

Men need to understand that a woman's brain is like a big plate of spaghetti. There are no boxes for individual noodles. Looking at it from above you can't tell where one begins and the other ends. This would make a man panic, but it's how a woman functions. It's all intertwined and everything is touching everything else. This is how the world makes sense to her.

You have probably had this conversation with your wife:

"Honey, what's up with the kids?"

"Oh, they're fine. And by the way, can you believe this? Mary told me as I dropped them off that the Hancock's are getting a divorce and the golf course is closing for the season and there's a new women's store in town. I was thinking maybe we should take the kids to the new McDonald's. I hear they have a great new play place. My mother hates those places—says they're a germ factory—but I think exposing kids to germs every once in a while will build their immune systems. Mom is coming for the weekend. You know, I told you that right before you left for work. Oh, that's right today is Saturday. You were leaving for golf. What did Stan wear? He always dresses so flashy for golf."

The guy's head is spinning as he frantically jumps from box to box, trying to follow his wife. Gentlemen, she does not talk like that to frustrate you. That's how her brain is wired. Everything leads to something else. Be aware of it and respectful that she functions that way. Just be happy you don't have to live in there.

Here's a suggestion, fellas, to help tame the senseless mass of noodles. Once a day, give your wife 15 minutes of uninterrupted conversation. No kids. No TV. No phones. Simply ask her, "How was your day?" Then listen as she unravels the spaghetti. You will be giving her a great gift.

Here are a few special "noodles" of spaghetti you men should be aware of:

- **The Comparison Noodle** -- Do not EVER compare your wife or any part of your wife's anatomy to another woman. This will send her into a tizzy like no other trying to figure out "...why you'd even look at Ann's hair." Especially do not compare her to any female members of her family; *especially* not her mother!

- **The Conversation Noodle** -- When you are having a conversation with her, whether trivial or important, she needs to feel as though she has your undivided attention. When you actively listen, it makes her feel loved and respected, and that what she has to say matters.

- **The Crazy Noodle** -- Yes, all women are a little bit crazy. You would be too if your brain never stopped thinking. They can't go to a "nothing box". As a result, they get overwhelmed with all that is coursing through their heads. This is where that 15 minutes a day will help. Giving her time everyday to process by having a conversation with you will keep the crazy noodle at bay.

- **The Romance Noodle** -- This one is huge. Your wife needs to know that she is still the only one you have eyes for. That she is still worthy of being wooed. That you know what she needs to feel loved. Here is some help if you are unsure: we recommend you read Dr. Gary Chapman's book, *The Five Love Languages*. Figure out your wife's love language and become an expert in that area.

- **The Children Noodle** -- Your wife is a mother from the moment your first child is born until...well, forever. She never stops being a mother to your children. She is still a mother when they leave the nest and have their own children. They are always her children, no matter what. Thus, she is always going to worry about them, think about them, and try to fix their problems. Just listen and offer help when asked.

- **The Hormonal Noodle** -- This is a dangerous noodle, and very real. Every 28–32 days your wife has to deal with a hormone dump that would cripple most men. This noodle floods her with emotions and thoughts that don't exist most of the time. When this noodle rears its head, you need to be kind, loving and compassionate. She's feeling awful and needs your reassurance that you love her dearly.

The Personality Factor

Hey there, it's me, Brooke. My husband and I have learned over the last 13 years that we have known each other, that our different personalities greatly affect how we interpret the world around us. I see life through Brooke-colored glasses. He sees life through his Pablo-colored glasses. Even though we are looking at the same thing, we both have a very different picture of it.

For example, Pablo is an easy-going guy. He's laid back, go-with-the-flow, he doesn't make waves. I, however, am a dreamer and a planner. I decide what I want to do, and then I start working backward, thinking through all the steps that it will take to reach my goal. What he might see as an immovable obstacle, I see as a puzzle that I haven't solved yet. I can be very determined, and very creative about the way I pursue the things that I want. When I decide that I am going to make something happen, I can be obsessive about it.

For a long time I have wanted to free range my backyard flock of chickens. It gives me joy to watch them wander around the yard, foraging for tasty treats and doing what God designed them to do.

Unfortunately, where we live near the woods and open farm fields, we have a fox problem. Foxes are cunning predators, and once they get a taste of your chickens, they will come back every night until your coop is empty. So, day after day, my hens remain locked in their safe, predator-proof coop, unable to run around and forage.

Well, this spring, I was determined that I would beat the fox and be the master of my chicken's destiny. I built a small, mobile chicken coop that I thought would keep the fox out, I parked it in the field behind my house, and began letting the birds out during the day. I immediately enjoyed watching them peck and scratch around the barns and paddocks as I went about my chores. It wouldn't last long.

The very first night a bird was stolen, right through a hole in the wire mesh floor of the coop. Lesson learned. I fixed the problem, but the fox had tasted blood and he would be back. The next night, a baby chick was taken from his brooder. Slick fox. The brooder was better secured the next day.

Then, the clincher. The fox snuck into my yard, just feet from my house, and stole two hens from their coop while they slept. Bold fox! Ooooh, he made me so mad.

This was war, and I was determined to win. I secured the birds the best I could. I bought a radio to fill the yard with noise during the night, and did a little target-practicing. The next day, I set my alarm for four O'clock in the morning. By 4:15, I was standing at my kitchen window, a cup of coffee in hand, waiting.

I dare you.

Sure enough, there he was. He came in the last few minutes of darkness, when only one side of the sky is faintly blue. I watched him stalk through the yard, straight to the coop full of sleeping birds.

I don't know what I had planned when I barged out the kitchen door in a bathrobe and pajamas, my empty coffee mug my only weapon, but thankfully the sound of the back door was enough to send him packing. Battle won, for now. I would meet him again tomorrow.

My determination paid off in the end. A solid week of 4am wake up calls and fast breaks into the yard convinced him that my chickens weren't worth the effort. Turns out my aim isn't too great. Meanwhile, Pablo looked on, mildly amused at the lengths I was willing to go to find safe pasture for a motley group of chickens. We see things differently. I don't expect him to understand. He gives me the grace to be who I am. He entertains my crazy ideas and even helps me flesh them out when he can.

Jay and Laura will tell you that they see things differently, too. Laura is a glass-half-full kind of person, where Jay tends to have a more pessimistic outlook. Personality clashes are to be expected in marriage. We are each looking at life through our own individual lens.

We Think About Different Things

One of our favorite mantras is *if it's important to your spouse, it should be important to you.* I (Jay) remember early in our marriage when all Laura wanted to do was go to the mall and shop. Ugh. First, I'd rather be outside playing golf. Second, there are so many people in malls. They crowd this claustrophobic human. Third, it takes MONEY to shop. Have I mentioned I'm a bit of a tightwad?

So without fail, every time we would go shopping, I'd make it my duty to make sure Laura knew I was not having fun. In fact, sometimes I would actually make the experience miserable. I know, I'm a horrible husband—but I can be educated.

A couple times a year we host the Celebrate Your Marriage Conference at Grand Hotel on Mackinac Island, MI. While Laura and I are speakers at the event, we always enjoy hearing from the guest speakers and learning from their message. I distinctly remember the first time we brought in Dr. Gary Chapman, author of *The Five Love Languages.* Laura and I had taken the test and knew our love languages, and we were very excited to hear him speak. I'll never forget his words that day.

"I loathe going to the mall with my wife," he said, "It's the last thing on earth I want to do. But, I have to remind myself, *if it's important to her it should be important to me,* so I go with a smile on my face."

Ouch, right through the heart. I was convicted beyond measure. Marriage isn't all about me. I should care about the things that Laura cares about. Now, when she says she wants to go shopping, I smile. "That sounds like fun," I will say.

The key is to watch how much joy it brings your spouse. When

I see how much fun Laura is having, it makes my day. I've now applied this same principle to watching HGTV or the Food Network, having 18 pillows on our bed because it "looks pretty," and a whole plethora of things that bring her joy.

Men Think About Facts and Activities

Laura here. It goes without saying that the same applies to us ladies. If it's important to your husband, it should be important to you. Don't let your eyes glaze over when he starts rattling off his favorite football teams stat lines for the season, or when he wants to tell you every shot he made on every hole on the golf course. These are the facts and activities that are important to him, so they should matter to you.

His brain is wired to think in terms of facts. It's why he is logical. It's why he tries to fix things when all you want him to do is listen. He listens to the facts then draws a logical conclusion on how to solve the problem.

The way he's wired is also why he loves activities. Shoulder to shoulder is how men bond with each other. That's why it's important for your husband to have golfing buddies or fishing buddies or his bowling league. When you let him go and bond with his buddies, then give him the chance to come home and tell you how Brad almost fell out of the boat, you will be connecting with him on a deep level.

We were watching an episode of *Island Hunters* on HGTV last night. *Island Hunters* is basically wealthy people looking to purchase a private island, either for a private retreat or for investing in a resort. It's nothing we could or would ever do, but it is fun to watch.

On one particular episode, a couple was looking to spend up

to 10 million on an island. She wanted a private retreat and he wanted an investment property. The realtor showed them one of each. Of course, that made their decision very difficult, as they each wanted what they wanted.

As they were discussing their options, the man kept hounding his wife. "What do you think? What do you think?" he kept asking.

She just looked at him, eyes glazed over, unable to respond. For her, it wasn't about thinking. It was about feeling. The investment property had her feeling overwhelmed. It was too big and too much to manage. The private island, however, left her feeling relaxed and serene. The decision for her was based on those feelings.

For him, the investment island was just what tourists wanted when visiting the Carribean. It was cheaper than the private island. It would more than pay for itself. For him the decision was based on those facts.

What is a wealthy couple who can't agree on which Island to buy to do? Why, buy both, of course!

Women Think About People and Feelings

If it's important to your wife it should be important to you. She's primarily thinking about people and feelings. So don't let your eyes glaze over when she comes home from lunch with her BFF and she wants to tell you all about so-and-so, and how Susie got her feelings hurt when Jane showed up in the same outfit.

She's wired to think about people. It's the nurturer in her. That's why she wants to make sure everyone has had enough

34

to eat and enjoyed the meal. It's why some women wear themselves out trying to please everyone and they don't take care of their own health.

Women "feel" all the time. She attaches a feeling to everything from how she feels about her haircut to how her outfit looks, and why the burrito is making her feel bloated.

We have a perfect example of how a husband and wife can think about one situation in two totally different ways.

I (Jay) was invited to go on a pheasant hunting trip to South Dakota with some buddies. I'm not much of a hunter, but my Grandpa on my mom's side was and he had left me a vintage 1953 Browning Lite 12. My buddies told me it would be some of the best guy time I'd ever have. Boy, were they right!

I flew to South Dakota and had the week of my life. You can't hunt pheasant until 10am in South Dakota, which meant we got to sleep in, eat a big breakfast, then practice shooting clay pigeons on the lodge's back 40.

Then we'd drop half the crew at one end of a corn field where they remained as blockers. The other half of us would be trucked to the other end of the field. We were the walkers. The concept is simple. As we walk the field, the pheasants run toward the blockers. Once the birds realize they can't run away, they take flight. That's when the fun begins!

The beautiful thing about pheasant hunting is you are supposed to make noise to scare the pheasants. So we'd talk about sports or some other guy talk, and we'd watch the bird dogs work their magic.

Afterward, we would return to the lodge for an amazing lunch.

We would go out in the afternoon to hunt some more. Then we would go back to the lodge, relax in the hot tub, have a huge dinner, and sit by the campfire and tell stories.

I remember one day we hit the mother load. We were in a field and, no lie, I'd take 5 steps and a bird would fly up right in front of me. Five more steps and—boom! Another one bites the dust. Five more and again, dead pheasant. It was such an adrenaline rush.

We limited out by lunch, so we spent the afternoon at a gun and axe throwing range. We shot every kind of gun imaginable and had an axe throwing contest. It was pure Heaven on earth. I couldn't wait to go home and tell Laura about every bird I shot and every great meal I devoured.

I walked in the door ready to tell my tales when Laura interrupts me.

"I want to hear it all, I really do, but first tell me what did it feel like?" she asked.

"What do you mean?" I said.

"What did it feel like to go hunting?" she replied.

"It felt great! I shot my gun and pheasants died and then we got to eat them!"

Then Laura asked, "What did everyone wear? Were you warm enough? Did you stay dry?"

Huh?

Classic case. I wanted to talk about facts (how many birds I shot) and activities (all the fun we had) and she wanted to talk about people (what did everyone wear) and feelings (how did it feel to shoot a pheasant).

How We are Different is How We Look Like God

It says in Genesis when God created humankind, He made us in His image. It's commonly understood that we are creative because He is creative. We love beauty because He created and loves beauty. We have compassion because He is compassionate, and so many other traits. We look like Him. That is how He made us the same. He also made us different.

Men and Women both reflect the image of God, but we do it in markedly different ways. Generally speaking, men are tough, brave, push the limits, and enjoy a challenge. They were built to carry burdens and responsibilities that women would crumble under.

Also generally speaking, women are nurturing, compassionate, people oriented, and able to persevere through pain that would turn a grown man into a baby. In the areas where we are different, we also look like him.

Don't get us wrong, there are plenty of tough women and compassionate men, but most often, we reflect the image of God very differently. It's as if God took his heart, broke it into two pieces, and gave half to man and half to woman. The parts of your husband or wife that are foreign to you are a reflection of a small piece of God that you don't have. The ways that they are different from you is a way they look like God. Remember *that* the next time you want to go ballistic on your spouse for something you just don't understand. The beautiful part of this dichotomy is that when we come together as husband and wife in unity—the way God intended it to be—we get a more complete picture of the beauty of God.

Your Reflections

Is a light bulb coming on in your brain as you understand how different you and your spouse are mentally? Now we can move on to making that mental mess work in your marriage. Answer the following questions:

1. Do you and your spouse function differently? What examples can you see in your own relationship of the differences between men and women?
2. What are some of the ways that your spouse reflects God in your differences?

_____

_____

_____

_____

_____

_____

_____

_____

Chapter 3

We Must Mentally Meld

How do we handle being so different on such a basic level as our thought life? How can we ever communicate effectively when he talks about facts and activities, and she talks about people and feelings? How will we ever understand each other when we can read or hear the same information and come up with totally different results? How do we get on the same page when mentally, we are both a mess? Well, we're glad you asked.

Melding is a Must

Our messy marriages can, at times, feel like we are combining oil and water. You can put oil and water in the same container. You can even stir them up together. Mixing, however, seems impossible. A husband and wife are in the same marriage, living in the same house, raising the same children, yet mixing seems impossible. No more attempts to mix. *Melding* is the way to take those mental differences and begin to make the most of them.

The term *meld* came about in the 1930's and 40's. It was new technology—a mixture of melting and welding. It described the process of taking two elements and combining them so that they were so thoroughly mixed they could no longer be separated. Two unique substances become one, new substance, without either one losing any of its original properties. Sound familiar?

The bible talks about two things that are a mystery, and only two. The first is the relationship between Christ and the church. That's why no one will ever "figure out" the church. God created a mystery and that's just the way it will be. The second thing the bible calls a mystery is a marriage. Your marriage is a mystery that is being discovered and explored piece by piece over a lifetime. For all of us type A personalities that want to find the right answer, sorry! There's no right answer. It's a never-ending journey where we learn, grow, face challenges and overcome them. The further we walk, the more of the mystery we unravel.

When we allow God to work in our marriages, he melds us into one new, amazing and useful tool that didn't exist before, without either of us losing what makes us an individual. We have found a few simple things that help us to meld. We snuck them into this sweet little acronym to help you remember.

M—mind your spouse's business
E—enjoy the differences
L—love the struggle
D—do not conform

Let's unpack those a bit more.

Mind Your Spouse's Business

We mentioned in the last chapter that a phrase we repeat a lot is *if it's important to your spouse, it should be important to you.* We often say this to couples who are struggling to find common ground in their marriages. They have different interests, hobbies, activities, priorities, skills, or whatever, and don't feel like they have a lot in common. They are forgetting that common ground is built, not found.

For example, Jay loves golf. I (Laura) was not a golfer when we first met. My dad played golf. I watched golf on TV, but I had never played myself. I was more into playing team sports like soccer and softball. I soon realized, however, that by maintaining that I had no interest in golf, I was missing out on a huge way that I could connect with Jay. I resolved that I would take an interest and learn a little bit about it, just to show him I care.

Jay's golfing buddies all had wives who wanted to learn to play golf, too. We had all discovered that if we wanted to spend time with our husbands, learning to play golf was the way to go. So we set out to learn. Now, a little tip here for you women who may want to learn to play golf: do not, under any circumstances, allow your husband to teach you. Talk about messy!

Instead, all of us girls went to golf school. It was like a girl party on the golf course for an entire week! It was a lot of laughter, eating, socializing, and...oh yeah we learned to play golf, too. I learned that I actually enjoy golf. Now it is something that Jay and I do together. We found common ground in our relationship because I was willing to take an interest in something he likes.

It's fantastic when you discover something you equally enjoy, but that may not happen for all of your interests. That's ok. You may never decide you really enjoy his hobby, and there's nothing wrong with that. You don't have to pretend you do. In fact, *don't* pretend that you do. Just asking a few questions and listening to your spouse talk about his or her passions will ignite a connection. You can enjoy your spouse's delight at you taking an interest in something important to him or her.

For example, I LOVE to shop. It is a fact that I will probably state a few more times before you are done reading this book. Jay puts up with it because he knows how much I love it. He will accompany me to the mall, walk with me, hold my shopping bags and listen to me go on and on about this pair of shoes or that super funky necklace. I don't even mind it when he sits in the man chair outside the store. In fact, he loves it when he finds a man chair. He loves it even better when he finds one *inside* the store so he can approve what I am purchasing. Approving isn't about the money. It is about how something looks on me.

"No one wants you to look more beautiful than I do!" he will say. Translation? *Take that shirt off. It makes you look like a box!*

He doesn't enjoy it anymore than he did when we were first married, but he shows me that he cares by being there with me and holding my hand. Start by caring about it just because it's important to your spouse and see where it takes you.

Enjoy the Differences

There's a myth going around that *compatible* is synonymous with *same*. You like the same things, you think the same way, you read each other's minds. That's true compatibility. No. That's boring! I've said it before at our speaking events, if you were both the same, one of you wouldn't be necessary. You're different on purpose because you each bring something important to the table.

Our co-author, Brooke, has an interesting perspective on the differences in a husband and wife, and the richness they can bring to a marriage. She was raised on a farm in rural southern Delaware, full of small towns and country living. Her husband, Pablo, was raised in the bustling metropolis of Pachuca City, Mexico. When they first met in college, they didn't even speak a common language. Then they fell in love.

Pablo's small family is quiet, soft-spoken, introspective and calm-natured. Brooke's very large family is loud, nosey and loves to gather, play games, and interact with each other. While Pablo is patient and calm, Brooke can be outspoken and forward when she wants to. Pablo is techy and loves gadgets and devices. Brooke is earthy and loves plants and animals. Even their spiritual backgrounds are very different. In Pablo's Mexican culture, the spiritual world is open and very much accepted, where Brooke's upbringing was very conservative in that regard. They couldn't be more different.

It's easy to look from the outside and say—as some did—that their relationship would never work; they are just too different. But they learned each other's languages, fell in love with each other's cultures, and learned to look past their many differences to how God can grow them as individuals through those differences.

Pablo and Brooke are still married today, not because they are special in some way from the average couple, but because they accepted the very obvious differences in themselves, and *learned to enjoy them*. Instead of trying to change your spouse to be more like you, look at his or her differences as an asset. It's a valuable trait or habit that you don't have, but you have access to because you are united as one.

Brooke will tell you that being married to Pablo has been

infuriating at times. She makes decisions quickly and is ready to move forward right away. Pablo is not that way. He prefers to take time, think through all the options and repercussions before making a decision. While this can drive her up a wall, she sees how they have avoided disaster because of this habit. She has learned to slow down and wait on God through Pablo's example.

You and your spouse are no different. You each have strengths and weaknesses, and the more different you are, the more likely that you actually complement each other in some way. Learn to see those differences, appreciate them, and enjoy them.

Love the Struggle

I (Jay) relate a lot of life to the game of golf. I'm also a former Chaplain for the PGA, so I love golf quotes. One of my favorites is from Tommy Armour. He says about golf, "You've got to learn to love the struggle." That is great news, isn't it? I'll bet that really gets you pumped up. But if you golf, you understand that golf is hard. It's a struggle.

There is a sign behind the reception desk at Doral Country Club in Florida that says:

Golf is like love. If you're not serious, it's no fun. If you are serious, it will break your heart.

This is where we find ourselves when we look at marriage. You have to put your whole heart into it in order to reap the rewards.

There's a psychological term called the 7-year-itch, which says that happiness in a relationship tends to decline around seven years in. Around the seven-year-mark, things begin to fall apart. It's when many couples "fall out of love" and decide to walk away.

There's all kinds of marriage advice out there on how to know if your marriage will stand the test of time. You can read blogs and take quizzes until Jesus comes back. The problem here isn't a lack of love, or sexual fulfillment, or healthy conversation. It's the fact that as humans we just don't like to struggle. It isn't fun. When things get hard—and they always do—we start looking around for someone to blame, someone to rescue us, some excuse to get out of the struggle.

It was right around 7 years for us when we suddenly realized the permanence of this marriage we had created. We were in this together and we couldn't get out. It was either call it quits or renew our commitment to making the marriage work. So we learned to love the struggle. It's a struggle that brings so many sweet rewards if you are willing to persevere through it.

Like golf, when things are not going your way, you can blame the club, you can blame the weather, you can blame the caddy and give up. Or you can press in and reach the satisfaction of having overcome the obstacles in your way. Silly me, I can vividly remember in my 20's thinking that life and marriage have to get easier at some point, right? No, every stage of life has its challenges.

Newlyweds -- Learning to live with this one you love.
Married with babies -- Will we ever stop changing diapers?
Married with kids -- Will we ever stop being a taxi?
Married with teens -- Bigger kids bigger issues!
Empty Nest -- Who is this person in my bed?
Elderly -- I can't hear you or see you, but my nose tells me it's you.

On top of these normal stages of life, many couples will also deal with illness, job loss, aging parents, re-locating, and other struggles. At the writing of this book Laura and I are empty-nesters. We couldn't be happier about this. We love our kids, but we raised them to move out. We're relatively young (just two kids at heart), we love our ministry, we love our ability to travel, we enjoy meeting amazing people, and the list goes on. But there are challenges. I have always struggled with my weight. Between our travel schedule and my ever slowing metabolism, it gets harder and harder to stay fit.

For Laura, the challenge is "the change". You know...menopause. When she was 12 or 13, women would tell her that a change was coming. It would be beautiful, they would say, and Laura would turn into a beautiful young woman. She did by the way. Laura is a little more sarcastic about this second change. She will comment about how everyone is talking about the change, but they don't say what you are changing in to. She will rub her chin like she has whiskers and say, "I'm changing into my FATHER!"

The Tickle Fight and the Grizzly Bear

I don't dream very often in my sleep. It's probably because I daydream so much! When I do have a dream at night, they are very vivid. I mean wake-up-in-a-cold-sweat, vivid. Usually the dream is triggered by some real life event that is happening to me while I sleep.

A little back story. Early in our marriage when we were feeling frisky but not so amorous we would have tickle fights in bed. We would spend 5–10 minutes trying to tickle each other. When we were done, lying on our backs, gasping for air, one of us would say, "Was it good for you?"

Now when we're feeling frisky but not so amorous we play rock, paper, scissors to figure out who has to get up and turn out the lights. So romantic!

One night, not too long ago, I was having a wonderful dream of Laura and I having a good old fashioned tickle fight. There must have been a huge grin on my sleeping face. Then, without notice, Laura rolled toward me. My fun dream turned into a nightmare as I was suddenly being mauled by a hot, sweaty grizzly bear. Ah, Menopause. It has me longing for the good old days of simple PMS.

Do not Conform to the Pattern of this World

Melding with your spouse doesn't come naturally. As humans living in a fallen world, we generally think about one thing and one thing only: ourselves. Instead, we have to retrain our minds to think about the person that God has given us to love, honor and cherish. We like to say, *it's not about thinking less of yourself, it's thinking of yourself less.*

What a key for marriage! Write that down and hang it on your wall, or put it on your fridge as a daily reminder to live selflessly.

Romans 12:2 holds the key to melding with your spouse.

> *"Do not conform to the pattern of this world, but be transformed by the renewing of your mind. Then you will be able to test and approve what God's will is—his good, pleasing and perfect will."*

The world around you will tell you that you need to get yours, look out for number one, take care of yourself first. After all, no one else is going to do it. But in God's world, the rules work differently. We are to place each other higher than ourselves, because *He* has promised to take care of us. That might seem a little upside down, and that's exactly right! He delights in confounding those who think they are wise, and giving unattainable wisdom to the simple.

We can't understand this principle using the world's logic. It makes no sense in the context of our fallen and broken world. That's why Paul says not to conform to this world's way of doing things. We have to have our minds transformed by renewing them in Christ. Then we can understand what God desires for our marriages.

If I Only Had a Brain

People think because we make people laugh and give marital advice that we must have a perfect marriage. Guess what? We do! A perfectly *messy* marriage. We argue *a lot*. We hurt each other *a lot*. And we don't see eye to eye *a lot*! What makes it perfect is that we are learning—present tense—that God gave us each other because He knew we needed each other.

We are both smart but in very different ways. We compliment each other's gifts. We've often said that between us we have just one brain. That's what happens when you put two half-wits together. What's worked for us is laughter. We laugh with each other, at each other, and make it a point to let those around us know it's ok to laugh, too. In fact, it's encouraged!

The winter solstice occurs during the hemisphere's winter. It is the day with the shortest period of daylight and longest night of the year. In the Northern Hemisphere, this is the December solstice, usually the 21st or 22nd of December.

Last December 21st, Laura sprung out of bed and declared, "It's the longest day of the year!"

I looked at her quizzically. She meant the *shortest* day of the year. Her eyes popped wide open when she realized her mistake. She rapped three times on her forehead with her knuckles.

"Hello, anyone home?" she mocked. Then we both had a good laugh about it.

Don't conform to the world's wisdom. It is foolishness. Learn to love the struggle; learn to live through it; learn to grow through it. Just because it gets *hard*, doesn't mean it's not *good*. Transform your thinking, and look at your marriage through *His* eyes. That is how we mentally meld.

Your Reflections

What are some ways you need to transform your thinking in regard to your marriage, so that you may mentally meld?

_____

_____

_____

_____

_____

_____

Chapter 4

We're all a Mess Emotionally

Emotions are part of life. We all have them. We all express them. Some hold them in until they are on their last nerve and then—boom! An explosion happens. All those emotions that they have been holding in finally come out. Others express their emotions the moment they feel them, with no filter and no regard for others. For others it is a slow drip; they express those emotions with no big explosion, in a matter-of-fact type of way. Then there are some who withhold their emotions entirely. They have blocked their feelings off from others so that it would seem they have none at all.

What makes an emotional mess in marriage is the fact that each of us express our emotions differently. If you take a good hard look at yourself and your spouse, chances are you can identity with one of the scenarios above. In our marriage, we relate to a few. At times, I (Laura) hold my emotions in until I explode. At other times, I am the matter-of-fact dripper. Jay, on occasion, will also hold his emotions until he explodes, which can make for some fun times in the Laffoon house. He can also express emotions the moment he feels them.

Watching TV is a way that we wind down at the end of the day. It's a habit we have developed as a result of working late and being in hotel rooms most weekends. The other night, Jay wanted to watch Undercover Boss. If you have never watched this show, the boss of a company or corporation disguises him or herself and goes undercover in the company to see how the employees are working and systems are functioning. The boss always hears stories from his employees that break his heart and cause him to do something for those in need. The end is always emotional. Most shows end with Jay and I tearing up. This night was no different. I don't remember what happened at the end of this particular episode, but I was bawling by the end. Jay looked at me funny.

"Why are you crying?" he asked.

I had tears rolling down my cheeks. "I am done with this show, I am tired of feeling. I really don't like to feel!"

You and your spouse are going to express your emotions in different ways. That's ok! That's actually healthy. We need to understand that if we are going to move toward making the most of the emotional mess in our marriages.

Jay's Day of Insensitivity

As a woman, it's easy for me to admit when I'm an emotional wreck, but we can sometimes forget that our husbands have those times as well. Between the two of us, Jay is the more sensitive one. Our kids know he's the nurturer. I'm the one who would say to them, "Suck it up, it's no big deal." It's just the way I am, or maybe the way I was raised. I am the third of four kids. I think by the time I came around, my parents were tired and overwhelmed. Their philosophy was that I should figure it out myself. I have tried to negate this philosophy in my own family, but sometimes I fall back on my family origins.

Each spring, just as it is getting warm in Michigan, we start thinking about getting our patio and porch furniture out. We usually take a Saturday and make a day out of setting it up. Well, on this particular Saturday morning, I woke up to Jay not talking at all. That's really unusual. Normally, when Jay wakes up, his lips start flapping. The night before, we had an argument, but I was pretty sure we had resolved it. He must just be really tired. I left it alone.

A little while later, I asked, "What are we going to do today?"

"Whatever."

Ok, whatever. I went about my day. I made breakfast. After about an hour, I asked my daughter Grace if she knew where her father went. Nope, no idea. I searched the whole house for him and did not find him. Finally, I did what any smart wife does in the digital age. I sent him a text message. "Where are you?" I asked.

"Out," came the reply.

"When will you be home?"

"Soon."

Ok. No big deal. A little later he walked in the door. "Do you want to go for a run?" I asked.

"Whatever."

At this point, I'm starting to pick up that he's still upset about something. I ran back in my brain through the argument we had the night before to see what I might have missed, and I figured it out. Somewhere in the argument, I had accused Jay of being too sensitive. So now, he was trying to be insensitive. And guess what? Two can play this game. I saw him putting on his running shoes, so I said, "I thought you weren't going running today?"

"Whatever."

Fine. I'll go let him run by himself. I'm not running today, and I don't care. I'm going to put the patio furniture out by myself. That will show him!

A few minutes later I was dragging patio furniture piece by piece out of the shed, alone. Had I been in my right mind, I might have asked my 17-year-old to help, but I was too busy trying to prove a point. I was going to do this by myself. When Jay got back from his run he saw the long, teak table in its place on the front porch.

"Huh, got the furniture out," he commented.

"Yeah, all by myself." I said, eyeing him. One of us was going to have to end this. It might as well be me. "I know what you're doing. You're mad about what I said, so you're trying not to be sensitive."

"That's right, I am. You said I'm too sensitive. So, here's my day to not be sensitive at all."

He can be such a mess sometimes. After we talked it over, he got over his mood and we made up. I decided I like sensitive Jay better. It works better in my world when I'm the only insensitive one.

She is Mean!

Jay here. Laura is definitely the insensitive one in our relationship. She can be downright mean! I'll explain. Some friends told us one day over breakfast about a guy who claimed he could predict how long your marriage would last simply by how you treat your spouse in his presence. My first thought was that his study could not be scientific. He would have to go to their house and see how they treat each other *at home.* That's when it really counts.

Case in point: Laura treats me fine in public, but at home she is mean. One morning I stumbled downstairs, barely awake. As I turned the corner into our kitchen, there was a bug on the floor between me and the coffee pot. I did what any sane guy saving his family from giant bugs would do. I stomped on it, chanting, "Die, bug, die!"

I was fairly certain it was now dead. I had just accomplished a heroic feat. I looked up at Laura, expecting to see a face full of gratefulness and adoration. Instead what I saw was Laura bent over, laughing hysterically. Tears were rolling down her face. *What in the … ?*

After she recovered, she informed me that it was not a bug at all. It was a loosely rolled pile of black string that resembled a bug. She left it on the floor to scare our daughter who also hates bugs.

"You just killed some string," she said, still laughing. See? She is mean.

Wired Differently

Laura again. Women usually get a bad rap when it comes to

emotions. Most of the time we are perceived as the more emotional of the two partners. But men's emotions can be just as messy as ours. The difference is in how we feel the emotions we have and how we express them. We are wired to process our emotions in different ways. Where women feel all the time, about everything, men do not.

Women have a feeling about everything they encounter. They have a feeling about the drapes, and how the teller at the bank spoke and your current financial situation and the kids school activities and what you will have for dinner. Everything she does or encounters throughout her day produces an emotion. It's part of how she interacts with her world.

For example, I hated the condition of our kid's bathroom. It wasn't their fault. It is a 30-year-old house, and things just get dingy. The bathtub was the worst. It had rust stains from hard water. The shower door would not come clean, no matter what product I used or how hard I scrubbed. I could not stand it any longer. Inside, I was feeling disgusted by this bathroom.

We called a company that specializes in refinishing bathtubs. It took them exactly 3 hours to make my bathtub sparking again! The door came off and they buffed out the rust stains. It didn't look brand new, which had me feeling a bit disappointed. However, it was a vast improvement, which had me feeling a ray of hope.

I promptly went out and bought a new shower curtain and chrome polish for the fixtures. This made me very happy about the future of this bathroom. When Jay's mom and sister came over for lunch, we took them for a tour of the new bath. The oooh's and aaah's made me feel quite satisfied.

"Did you paint the bathroom as well?" they asked. I hadn't,

but I was elated that they noticed how fresh and clean it looked.

I still need to find some little knick knacks and a new blind to make the bathroom perfect. I am feeling much happier about this room of my house, but I won't "love" it again until I have everything exactly how I want it.

If a man felt all that, he would shut down from emotional overload. A guy's brain doesn't process an emotion for every moment of every day. He can do something, speak to someone, or perform a task without feeling either happy or sad or frustrated or elated or … anything. He just did it. It was part of his day. However, when he does feel happy or sad or frustrated or elated, he feels the entire depth of that emotion. He doesn't just half-feel it. That's why he will go crazy when his team scores a touchdown. That's why he will throw something or slip an expletive when he can't figure something out that he's tinkering with. Or, if he's like Jay, he might have a ridiculously over-the-top reaction over nothing.

The Chili Incident

We have the privilege of working out of our house. This has its benefits and its drawbacks. Having an office in your home can make you never stop working. We have been down this road a few times. It can also be fun. Some days we don't get out of our pajamas until after noon! Jay might try to tell you that one benefit is getting to have "naked Tuesdays", but I will not allow that to happen in our house.

What *does* happen, and is a definite benefit, is homemade meals. As people who are on the road 75% of the time, we love to cook at home whenever we have the chance. One evening for dinner we made a big pot of homemade chili. We still use the same recipe from when we had kids in the house, so there were lots of leftovers for the next day.

Tomorrow arrived, as did lunch time. I told Jay I was going to the kitchen to put the leftover chili on the stove. As the chili was heating up, I decided to add some niceties to create a bit of atmosphere for later that evening. I put out some nice place mats, turned on some music, and lit some candles. What a nice lunch we were going to have!

I had taken so much time creating atmosphere that I forgot about the chili on the stove. Oops! I turned it off and begged it to cool down. After what I thought was plenty of cool down time, I called Jay down for lunch.

Side note: I am married to Mr. Tender Tongue.

Jay came downstairs and admired all the effort I had put into the lunch. I put his bowl of chili in front of him, not really seeing any reason to tell him it might be a tad warm. Oops again! He wrapped his lips around that spoonful of hot chili and immediately spewed it right back out, all over my beautifully set table. He then began to accuse me of trying to *kill* him with hot chili.

Seriously, kill you? Overreact much? Besides, there are a lot less messy ways to accomplish that.

As men and women—as different people—we are going to express our emotions differently. It goes back to how our brains are different at a biological level. The connections or "wiring" is set up differently in a man's brain versus a women's brain. We process our feelings and emotions in different ways and at different levels. One is not right or wrong. It's just different.

58

We Express Emotions Differently

In your marriage, one of you is most likely the one who holds in emotions and one of you lets them out. The mess happens because we don't identify who is who. The one who holds in emotions tends to think that the one who lets them out is always angry or hurtful. The opposite happens as well. The one who lets them out tends to think the one who holds them in is apathetic about everything. And so begins the emotional mess.

Early in our marriage, and at times still to this day, when Jay expresses his negative emotions, I have a tendency to think he is angry at me. This is not usually the case—except in the chilli incident. Something or someone would make him angry. When that emotion finally was expressed, it was directed towards me even though I was not the cause. I remember as a new wife wondering what it was I was doing to make him so mad.

I (Jay), as a newly married man, often wondered if Laura had any feelings at all because she never showed them. Little did I know, they were sitting just under the surface and would eventually reach a boiling point. A child would not obey. A friend went out with another friend for lunch and Laura was not included. The new pair of jeans she just bought didn't fit right. Then it was like I was being shot at with a machine gun. The negative emotions just kept coming at me and there was nothing I could do to stop them. I was not usually the cause of them, but I was definitely the recipient of the rage.

Understanding how your spouse expresses their emotions makes it easier to give each other grace and not take it so personally.

Your Reflections

Take time to think through how you process your emotions. How do you express them? How does your spouse express them? Write down some of your answers and discuss them with your spouse. This will allow each of you to remind the other that, 9 times out of 10, you are not the cause of the spewing of emotions.

_____

_____

_____

_____

_____

_____

_____

_____

_____

Chapter 5

Exercise Emotional Self-Control

One of the most grown up things you will ever have to do is take responsibility for your own emotional control. Hey folks, Brooke here.

My husband and I are raising a precious 3-year-old little girl with chocolate brown eyes and a head of curly hair. We are head over heels in love with her, but she is three. The nickname "three-nager" has never felt more appropriate than for this mini roller coaster of emotions. There's so much going on in that little head of hers that she still is not equipped to process, and it bubbles up to the point of exploding daily.

Part of our role as her parents is helping her think through and express all that she is feeling in a healthy way. It's exhausting! It requires all of the patience and intentionality I can muster. But we won't have to do this for her forever. At some point, as she matures into a healthy adult, she will assume responsibility for her own emotions. It's part of growing up. There's probably no better sign of a healthy, mature adult than good emotional self-control.

When we, as adult men and women, lack the skills to deal with what we are feeling, we are like overgrown toddlers throwing tantrums. It's not fun for anyone around us, and we look ridiculous while we're doing it.

Making the most of your emotional mess means exercising discipline over your emotions. Yes, discipline...as in, your emotions are under *your* control. It's not that you don't feel strong emotions. I'm not suggesting you should ignore or deny them. Deal with them maturely. Don't overreact. Make your emotions submit to and obey the truth. This is taking responsibility for your own emotional well-being.

My Response is my Responsibility

As a kid, I (Jay) overreacted to everything. My parents have told me that I would blow up over the littlest things, until they started teaching me that m*y response is my responsibility.*

I may still struggle slightly with overreacting as an adult. It is a beautiful summer day here in Michigan. We took our computers to the front porch to enjoy some sunshine as we write this manuscript. I wasn't out here long before a yellowjacket came poking around. My reaction to this creature flying around my head almost resulted in my computer being thrown down on the concrete front porch and glasses of tea flying out into the front yard. I am a work in process!

Learning that my response is my responsibility helped me understand that I was able to manage my emotional outbursts. It has also been beneficial in our marriage. Laura may say something hurtful to me, but I don't have to say something hurtful back. I have a responsibility to respond in a healthy, mature way.

Take the chilli incident from the previous chapter. Yes, the soup was way too hot. Yes, Laura could have—*should have*—warned me that it was too hot. Spewing the chilli out of my mouth was a natural reaction to heat. Accusing Laura of trying to kill me? Probably a bit of an overreaction.

I (Laura) exercised emotional discipline in the chilli incident. I will admit I should have warned him that the chilli might be tad hot. When the chilli was spewed all over my beautifully set table, my natural response would have been to get angry and blame him for ruining lunch. I held my tongue. The accusation of trying to kill him with chilli may have elicited a smirk from me, but again I held my tongue.

Recently our pastor defined self-discipline as *the ability to say no, when you have the right to say yes.* When we have been disappointed, hurt, angered, made fun of, mistreated, or mis-led and feel we have the right to retaliate in the same way, we must say no.

People are Like Garbage Trucks

Jay back with you. I took Laura on a surprise trip to New York City for her 50th birthday. While bouncing around the city seeing the sights, we met a really friendly taxi driver. This guy was not what I imagined a typical New York cab driver to be. We were making conversation and talking about sights we wanted to see in his beautiful city when another driver suddenly cut him off. Our driver had to slam on his breaks to keep from hitting the car in front of him. Then the guy who cut him off turned around and, with a flourish, flipped our driver the international finger of love and respect. I was expecting a colorful reaction from our guy, but much to my surprise, he didn't even beep the horn. He seemed to take it all in stride, and even offered a smile as he waved back at the guy.

"You're not what I expected from a New York cab driver!" I said, visibly surprised at his reaction.

His response was profound. "I've learned in my life that people can be like a garbage truck," he said. "People have so much junk on the inside they're just waiting to dump on whoever they can dump it on. So when I find a person like that, and I know they need a little bright side in their day, I'm going to try and give it to him. I don't know that guy's problems, I don't want to know that guy's problem, but obviously he has a lot of garbage on the inside when he cuts me off and flips *me* the bird. So, the next time someone dumps garbage on you," he says, catching my eye in his mirror, "just give them a little ray of sunshine back. They probably need it."

When I have a bad day, a little bit of garbage builds up inside me. If I'm not careful, I can spill it on Laura. We don't mean to do it to each other. We don't want to. It just happens. Exercising emotional self-control minimizes that. In fact, why don't you start a new tradition? From now on, whenever you have an argument or someone is having a bad day and dumping on the other one, just smile and wave and offer them a little sunshine. Just don't forget to duck the punch.

Each of us have to take responsibility for our own responses. I have no control over what Laura may say or do to me, but I do have control over my response.

Let Each Other Be Different

In addition to taking responsibility for your own response, re-member that you and your spouse will naturally have different emotional processes and expressions. We can and should give our spouses the freedom to express their emotions within the framework of their own personality.

We like to watch America's Got Talent. It's basically a contest

64

version of an old variety show. There's music, dance, magic, and feats of incredible human strength and agility.

In a recent episode Laura and I watched together, an awkward and petite 13-year-old girl came out on stage. She was visibly nervous as she answered the preliminary questions from the judges. Her hands were trembling in fear. When the music started, however, she completely changed. She must have forgotten about the crowd as she rocked the house with a soulful rendition of "I Put a Spell on You". I sat there in amazement as this tiny little girl belted out a powerful song. She received a standing ovation from all 4,000 people in attendance as well as the four judges. She was given four yes votes from the judges, moving her on to the next round.

I was filled with joy. I turned to Laura to say how amazed I was when I caught her wiping tears from her eyes.

"What's wrong?" I said.

"I'm sad she didn't get the golden buzzer," she replied.

A golden buzzer is like a trump card. When a judge hits this buzzer, it advances the contestant straight to the finals. Here I am about to shout with joy, and Laura is crying over the buzzer. Talk about different emotional responses!

Stan and Sue's Story

Stan and Sue had a death in their family. They experienced a loss no mom or dad want to have to endure. Their grief process was wrapped up in each of their personalities. Stan is an engineer. He is methodical and thoughtful. He did not want to go to counseling. Getting back to his routine is what allowed him to normalize and process his grief.

Sue's creative and verbal personality benefited from counseling. She wanted to express her grief to someone who could help her work through all the questions of her loss. Each allowed the other to grieve in their own way.

Whether it is grief, anger, hurt or disappointment, we have to allow each other to express our emotions within the bounds of our personality.

People Say the Darndest Things

Laura chiming in here. When you live out your marriage on stage, it makes for some fun comments from the audience. We hear things like:

"Oh my goodness, it's like you're a fly on our wall!"

"You guys are so real and relatable."

"We love your transparency."

We love getting real and honest feedback from our audience members, but the level of transparency we have on stage seems to make people feel comfortable making comments about our life and marriage that they probably shouldn't.

I was standing at the Compassion table at the conclusion of one of our Ultimate Date Nights when a woman approached me. She spent a few moments looking back and forth between the poster with our faces on it and me. It was really awkward. Then she put her hand on my shoulder and just patted me. "Good for you...Good for you," she said.

Apparently I had made some dramatic physical change since

the picture was taken. Maybe she thought I'd lost weight, or my hair was done differently. I don't know what she saw in the picture that was so wrong, but all I could do was stand there, dumbfounded. Thankfully my self-control kept my mouth in check.

Another time, another lady came up to me. "Laura, you look so pretty when you smile," she said.

Ouch! That hurt. I mean, I *try* to smile every second I'm on stage but there's a lot going on in my brain. I'm trying to remember lines and jokes, make people laugh, and make them think about their relationship all at the same time. And, yes, sometimes my feet are killing me from the fabulous shoes I'm wearing. Again, my self-control kicked in.

"Thank you," I said with a smile.

I'm usually very self controlled when women make comments like these because, well, it's what women do. We don't always realize how it comes across. When they start making comments about Jay, however, my self-control doesn't seem to kick in quite so quickly.

One recent example, a woman approached me at one of our Ultimate Date Night events. "How in the world do you put up with Jay?" she said. "He's so immature and nothing but a goofball."

I wanted to say, "You just spent 90 minutes laughing until your sides hurt. I know this because I saw *you* in the audience. That was because of Jay!" But I wasn't going to give her the satisfaction. I was not going to let her put my husband down. Instead, I leaned in a little closer. "It's the non-stop, mind-blowing sex!" I whispered.

I was quite proud of myself as I watched her jaw hit the floor. I guess there are times when losing myself control has been absolutely appropriate.

Two Powerful Phrases

Jay here. We have learned two very powerful phrases that help us keep communication open when emotions get high. The first phrase is, "Help me understand." A couple examples:

"Laura, *help me understand* why you threw out that last piece of pie." There is going to be some tension there when I have been thinking about that piece of pie all day long, then I come home to find it in the trash.

"It had mold on it."

Oh. If that's her response, then I guess instead of getting upset, I will thank her for saving me from eating moldy pie.

"Honey, *help me understand* why you're angry and it feels like you're angry at me?"

"I'm sorry. I'm not angry at you, we just lost a big client at work today and I feel responsible."

Using this one simple phrase can de-escalate rising emotions in a matter of seconds. The other powerful phrase is, "Do you know how _____ made me feel?" For example:

"Do you know how what you said about my dress made me feel?"

There are only two answers. Yes or no. My guess is his response will be no, which will allow you to tell your husband how his comments made you feel like the dress was ugly.

It is difficult to read some of the subtle nuances that drive the feelings of our spouse. Talking about it with words that de-escalate the situation, in addition to exercising emotional self-control, can help you communicate through the issue.

Like City Walls

Proverbs 25:28 says,

> *"Like a city whose walls are broken through is a person who lacks self-control."*

So many times for me, (Laura) exercising emotional self-control means taming my tongue. What is in my head comes out of my mouth before I even have time to think it through. I'm not really known for being sensitive with what I say. I have learned that a great way to exercise self-control over my emotions is to count to ten before I speak. Or 25. Or 100 — whatever it takes.

You have to figure out what it will look like in your marriage. Is it counting to ten? 100? Is it not taking every word that comes out of your spouse's mouth personally? I have to do this: I ask myself if Jay really meant what he just said the way it sounded. Probably not, so I choose not to take it personally.

Look at that scripture in Proverbs one more time. During the reign of the kings of Israel, when this scripture was written, the only time a city's walls were broken through was when it was conquered by a rival army. The scenes around the city after the walls had fallen would have been total chaos. There would have been killing, looting, robbing and raping —

devastation and destruction. A city's walls offered order and civility to the people living inside. They meant peace and safety. They were protection from anything outside that intended harm.

In a similar fashion, self-control is not keeping walls up between you and your spouse, but keeping the emotional chaos outside your marriage from wreaking havoc within. It is like a wall that surrounds your marriage, offering peace and safety from anything that desires to break in and destroy it. We all have emotional mess. Practicing healthy emotional self-control helps keep it in check, and keeps it from compromising your most precious relationship.

Your Reflections

What are some habits that you need to implement in your marriage to exercise emotional self-control?

_____

_____

_____

_____

_____

_____

Chapter 6

We're all a Mess Sexually

The show *Survivor* debuted when our son, Torrey, was 10. We had established a habit that we would watch a show of his choice every week together. When *Survivor* aired, this was the show he chose. Jay and I have remained loyal fans of the show long after Torrey outgrew his love for it. We have watched all 37 seasons to this point.

I think part of our love for this show is the fact that we could never do any of what the contestants are required to do. No showers for 39 straight days. Stand on a narrow piece of wood while balancing 3 balls in the middle of some round disk in 100 degree heat. Sleep on cutdown trees roped together to make a hut. Huddle in said hut during a typhoon with people you have just met. Eat creatures I have never heard of before. Lie boldly to people. Befriend people only to stab them in the back and vote them off the island. Yeah, some things we could never do, but we love to watch others do it! Recently we were watching the 37th season, commenting on the beauty of Fiji.

"Isn't Fiji where they have those beautiful resorts built out over the water?" I said to Jay.

He replied with, "You know, I think I could play *Survivor*."

"Really?" I said back. "You can't even eat pizza without folding the slice so you don't get your hands messy. You *really* think you could play *Survivor*?"

He thought about it for a moment. "I could play *Hotel Survivor*. They should make that show. You have to spend 39 days in a hotel. Eating out every meal. Having someone clean your room and make your bed. You get to take as many showers as you want. The games for rewards and immunity can be played around the city where the hotel is located. I am going to email Jeff Probst and tell him my idea."

I was about to burst his bubble. "Honey, we already play *Hotel Survivor*. It is our job—the Ultimate Date Night Tour with Jay and Laura Laffoon!"

"Oh right. I thought it sounded familiar."

You'd think that our traveling lifestyle, staying in lots of hotel rooms in many different cities, and talking to people about sex on a regular basis would mean we have an amazing sex life. Well think again. We'll be the first to confess, it's a struggle. We, too, are a mess sexually.

All That and a Bag of Chips

At the end of the day, we land in our two person chair. It is not a love seat but rather a chair built for two. It makes for great cuddling while we wind down with a TV show or two.

We have a wide variety of favorite shows, from *Blue Bloods* to *Diners, Drive-ins, and Dives*. One night we were watching a "shoot 'em up" show, as we call them. There was gunfire happening, bombs exploding, trucks catching fire, and of course, a ruggedly handsome hero. When one very tense scene ended, I

72

let out a sigh of relief.

"Wow!" I said, referring to the tense situation.

Jay thought I was referring to the ruggedly handsome hero. "Hey," he called, "I am all that *and* a bag of chips! But mostly just the chips."

I couldn't contain my giggles. After all these years, he still makes me laugh. Even though he totally misunderstood the reason for my sighing, Jay wasn't offended. We have learned a lot over the years, and learned to let a lot go. There are moments in marriage where a simple misunderstanding escalates sexual tension between a husband and wife. It's a real thing, even in marriage. Sexuality is messy and unpredictable.

Were all Messed Up

We're all messed up when it comes to sex. My father was a youth minister for 40 years before he retired. He shepherded children through their teen years into adulthood. He believed if a kid was mature enough to ask a question, they were mature enough to hear the answer.

When our son was about 4-years old, he ran out into the yard to see his grandpa.

"Hey grandpa," he said. "What's couple sex?"

My dad, in his infinite wisdom, thought since Torrey asked the question, he was ready to hear an answer—the *real* answer. So he began to explain to my four-year-old son all the aspects of human sexuality. As you can imagine, my son's eyes popped open. He couldn't believe this.

When my dad got done explaining, he asked, "Now do you understand?"

"Yeah."

"Why did you ask?"

"Because grandma said dinner would be ready in a couple secs."

Good job, Dad. Our son is now scarred for life! No wonder we're all messed up. Someone in our lives got things *really* wrong. Sexuality is messy and unpredictable.

True Love Waits...Or Doesn't It?

Our son is now grown and married. We actually knew his wife, Shana, long before he did.

Years ago, at our Ultimate Date Night Events, we would ask folks to fill out little forms with their contact information to be entered into a contest to win free books and DVD's. At the conclusion of the intermission, we'd select a few couples to win a book or DVD. Now we have moved into the 21st century and use texting. But back in the day, we would end each weekend with a stack of forms that needed to be entered into our database.

We asked ourselves who would want to do this tireless, thankless job? College students! So we asked Mitch Sheehan, who directed the college ministry at our church, if he knew of someone responsible that we could pay to enter these names every week.

Without missing a beat, he said, "Shana Dodge! She's smart,

responsible and a hard worker."

So we contacted Shana, set up an interview and were duly impressed. She was sharp! As soon as she left the office Laura looked at me. "Why can't Torrey meet a girl like her?" she complained. She then proceeded to play matchmaker, which made our son incredibly incensed. Moms, never play matchmaker for your kids! Even though you have the best of intentions, it will not be well received.

But I digress....

We had a great system in place. We'd drop the forms off at church on Tuesday morning and Shana would pick them up Tuesday night at U-life, our college student ministry. We started this in September of 2011 with the beginning of our fall Ultimate Date Night tour.

The next May we had forms to be processed from our Celebrate Your Marriage Conference held at Grand Hotel on Mackinac Island, Michigan. We had arrived home late Tuesday and didn't have time to leave the forms at church so we asked Torrey if he'd take the forms to U-life and give them to Shana Dodge.

"How do you know Shana Dodge?" he snapped back.

"She's been working for us since September."

"Oh."

The next week Torrey came to us Tuesday afternoon and with a sheepish look on his face.

"Do you have any more forms for me to take to Shana?" he asked.

"Sorry, bud. We're done with the tour until fall."

That August, Torrey and Shana were invited to a leadership retreat for U-life. A group of about 10 students, along with Mitch and his wife Makenzie, went away to a cabin for the weekend to plan out the next year of ministry to Central Michigan University students. That's where it all began, as they say. They didn't officially start dating until a month later, but it was obvious they were in love.

They approached us in January of 2013, fifteen months after Shana started working for us and four months after they started dating. We were not surprised by what they came to talk to us about.

"We're getting married," Torrey said.

"Fantastic! We couldn't be happier for you!"

"But we're both in our junior year and we can't decide if we should get married this summer, or wait until we've both graduated."

Ah, the conundrum. We knew they would have to pick their poison, so we laid it out openly for them. "It's your choice and we will support your decision either way," we explained. "However, you need to understand that you will face one of two very different challenges depending on your choice. If you get married this summer, before you graduate college, chances are you will face some financial pressure. If you wait until next summer you will face sexual pressure. Which would you rather deal with?"

Without missing a beat, they both said, "This summer it is!"

"I'll live off Ramen noodles and the occasional trip to Grandma's house," Torrey added.

So that July we had a wedding. Sexuality is messy and unpredictable!

A side note to the singles out there. Yes, true love is willing to wait. It's willing to delay gratification in order to gain the true prize. However, true love also has the wisdom to know when it's setting itself up for failure. Long engagements may work for some, but for others, once you know you've found the one you want to spend the rest of your life with, it may be smarter to go ahead and make the wedding commitment to one another.

What Do You Crave?

Take a moment right now to picture in your mind something you crave. A craving, as defined by dictionary.com, is *a powerful desire for something*. When you crave something, you deeply desire it. You think about it over and over. You obsess over it. It comes back to your mind again and again, even when your not actively thinking about it.

Guys, I (Laura) would imagine that you pictured your wife, or maybe a hobby you enjoy. For the women, I'm guessing you are picturing some kind of food. Chocolate or strawberries... or chocolate covered strawberries! We have lots of experience with cravings. Whether it is chocolate, ice cream, chips, or coffee, we know its power. There doesn't have to be any specific reason for it; although, at times, we can attribute it to biology. I will admit that I have used that one to my advantage!

"Jay, I need something salty. Maybe some chips. Yes, I need chips."

"Really? You *need* chips?"

"Yes! It's that time of the month, and *I want chips!*"

If you have been pregnant, you have probably experienced strange cravings for no reason at all. When I was pregnant with our oldest, I craved pizza all the time. Morning, noon, and night, I could not get enough pizza. Pizza was all I thought about. We would drive by Pizza Hut, I could smell the pizza. I could taste the pizza. I wanted the pizza. That might be why, to this day, our first-born loves pizza!

Here's a question for us all to ponder, ladies. How often do you crave your husband like you crave food? When was the last time you felt that powerful desire or yearning for him, sexually?

You probably felt that yearning while you were dating or engaged. You probably felt it quite a bit in the early days of your marriage. I wouldn't be surprised if somewhere along the way, that craving began to fade. Maybe it was after a big fight. Maybe his words have hurt you a few times. Kids came and now you are always tired. Maybe you haven't felt that desire in a long time. Maybe it's time to rekindle that craving.

Guys, have you stopped letting your wife know that you crave her? That you desire her? Have you stopped telling her how beautiful she is? Have you let her know lately that your desire is only for her?

If your wife is dismissive of these compliments, don't be discouraged. As women, we are reminded every time we look in the mirror that we no longer look like the woman you married. Our bodies have changed. We have a pudge where there was once flatness. A few more wrinkles and gray strands of hair show up every day. And the chin hairs... oh my!

The changes in our body make us feel less desirable. This feeling causes us to dismiss the attempts you make to let us know you still crave us. But don't give up! Keep letting her know you crave her. Sexuality is messy, but she desires—and needs—your persistence.

Sex Is Good!

We have a generation of adults who do not understand what great sex is in marriage. These adults grew up in a culture of *True Love Waits* and *Kiss Dating Goodbye*. These are great programs that promote sexual purity to teenagers. However, it seems the concept 'wait for sex until you are married' didn't translate to 'it is okay to have sex once you are married'. We deal with couples from this generation all the time who seem to have no idea that God created sex to be *enjoyed* between a husband and a wife.

What I (Laura) have discovered in talking to women from this generation, is that for the 8-10 years they were told to wait until marriage, what they were hearing was *sex is dirty*. Maybe the fault was in the deliverer of the message, or perhaps in their own immature and impressionable minds. The result was that they buried their sexual feelings deep as teenagers. When they get married, they just can't come to grips with sex as a beautiful and godly expression of love between a husband and wife. This has created countless couples who have no sex life in their marriage, or see it as an obligation rather than something God intended for them to enjoy.

This is why a man leaves his father and mother and is united to his wife, and they become one flesh. Adam and his wife were both naked and they felt no shame." –Genesis 2:24-25

Look at those phrases. United to his wife. Become one flesh. Naked and unashamed. God created husband and wife to have sex. There is no shame in marital sex. Sex is the ultimate connection a wife has with her husband and a husband with his wife.

"How beautiful are you, my darling! Oh how beautiful!
Your eyes are doves.
How handsome you are, my beloved! Oh how charming!
And our bed is verdant."
–Song of Song 1:15-16

"I am my beloved's and his desire is for me." –Song of Songs 7:10

The Song of Songs is about the sexual union of a husband and wife. Included in the verses is love, desire, sexual satisfaction, adoration and delight in each other. Look at the first passage above. Do you know what *verdant* is? It is a grassy field of rich vegetation. These two are making love in a field! Not my idea of fun, but whatever floats their boat.

In the record of creation in Genesis, each time God created something He took a step back, assessed it, and then pronounced, "It is good." God created sexual intimacy between a husband and wife. It is part of his creation, and it is good! It is to be enjoyed, to bring satisfaction to both husband and wife, and to create a bond between them that cannot be broken.

Sexuality is messy and unpredictable. Our culture, our parents, our churches, and we ourselves have all contributed to this mess. We can make the most of this mess and enjoy what God has created for us to enjoy.

Your Reflections

Ask your spouse this question: what can I do to bring more satisfaction to our sex life?

_____

_____

_____

_____

_____

_____

_____

_____

_____

_____

Chapter 7

Learning to Love

Jay and I travel about 10 months out of the year. Needless to say, it's a struggle to maintain good habits like exercising and eating healthy. We try to eat a good breakfast and a healthy lunch. Most nights after a show, we hit a grocery store for a pre-packaged salad and maybe some chicken tenders. Exercise rooms in hotels are not always the best, so we usually find ourselves at a park or mall, depending on the weather, to get in our steps. We do the best we can while we're on the road.

We ended our winter/spring tour of 2019 in the worst shape of our lives. It was time to get serious about getting healthy. We can't perform if we can't breathe! We joined a local gym that has a pool. We walk, bike, and now have taken up swimming. We also enjoy cooking. It is one of our favorite activities to do together.

Cooking a healthy meal takes planning and effort, but it is an important way that we invest in our health when we are able to. Pro tip: we recently joined a food subscription service that is low in calories but still packs in the flavor. We get to cook together, but someone else has thought it all out for us. Win-win!

We have also started using an app to track our food intake and exercise. It takes the thinking out of it, and it is helping us stay on track toward our fitness goals. Recently, as we were getting ready to go to the gym, Jay looked at me with his mischievous smile. I knew some silly remark was coming.

"So," he said, "I was on the app to see which exercise burns the most calories. We can either swim and burn 400 calories, or we can have sex and burn 60. You choose."

"Why can't we do both?" I asked.

"Honey, I am over 50!" he replied, "I can either swim *or* have sex, not both."

Overcome the Mess with L-O-V-E

Making the most of our sexual mess requires sexually submitting to each other. I am a word person. I love to take a word and go to the thesaurus to see what words are similar. It helps me gain a better understanding of it. I did this with the word submit. It is a word that we don't like to hear so much, right? It immediately brings up negative connotations, like master, servant, slave, inferior, superior, etc. However, when I went to the thesaurus and applied similar words to our thoughts of sexually submitting, here is what I came up with: **acknowledge** your spouse's sexual needs, **agree** to meet each other's needs, **surrender** to the needs of your spouse, **indulge** in the gift God created for you and your spouse.

Acknowledge. Agree. Surrender. Indulge. None of these bring to mind negative images. Rather, I see a beautiful picture of what God designed for husband and wife to enjoy. We can do this by learning to **L-O-V-E**: **L**earn your spouses sexual needs, **O**penly discuss your sex life, **V**ow to meet your spouse's needs, and **E**njoy the gift God has created for you as husband and wife.

Learn your Spouse's Sexual Needs

In doing research for this book, we learned that there was an ancient Hebrew law that allowed a woman to divorce her husband if she wasn't satisfied in the bedroom. If her husband were a selfish lover, she could send him packing. He didn't just have to complete his manly duty, he had to *satisfy* her. That's a tall order. Is that really fair to the guy? I (Jay) say it is, because men and women are aroused differently.

Men, let me ask you a question. How long does it take you to get aroused sexually? Most men respond with a snap of the fingers. I have heard it compared to a microwave. Just push the right button and we are ready to go. I am in my 50's now and that's still the way it works. Women, however, are different.

We have a friend, Dr. Michael Sytsma, who is America's leading Christian sex therapist. We learned from him that there is study after study that shows that it takes about 20 minutes for your wife to become sexually aroused. That's 20 minutes of back rubs, foot massages, and kissing. No, that doesn't mean you can go set a timer. It does mean that you need to slow down and take your time. Your wife needs that from you.

How we are aroused is different too. Our responsibility, men, is to invest the time in romancing and arousing our wives so that they can experience full sexual satisfaction in the bedroom. Women need affection to become aroused. Hand holding, kissing, back rubs, shoulder rubs, and the like are what arouses a woman. In other words, foreplay! To do any less is to be a selfish lover. The biggest pushback I get here is that there is

85

just not enough time. I hear all the excuses. The kids went to bed late. It's 11 o'clock. I have to go to work in the morning. Listen, we are here to meet each other's needs and sexually submit to each other. I promise you, gentlemen, it is worth it. It is not just having sex; it is *making love.*

The caveat, men, is that what turns your wife on changes, sometimes on a daily basis. What worked last time might not work this time. You have to hunt for what she's in the mood for each and every time.

Early in our marriage, I was informed that "groping" is NOT affection and that it actually has the opposite effect on Laura's desire to have sex. I would frequently try to be playful with her but before you know it, the testosterone would have me...well, groping. She'd get mad, then I'd get mad that she was mad, when all I was trying to do was get her motor running.

Because I love her and genuinely want to make love to her, I have learned over the years not to grope. It's a turn-off for her... most of the time. I'll never forget the words that came out of her mouth one night not so long ago.

We were newly empty-nesters and were enjoying life as just the two of us again. We were standing at the kitchen counter chopping up veggies for a salad when Laura turned to me.

"Why don't you grope me anymore?" she asked.

What!?

I almost dropped the knife I was holding. For decades she asked me *not* to grope her and now she's asking why I *don't* anymore? I was so confused. The look on my face must have said it all. She just shrugged her shoulders.

"Aren't I the mysterious one?" she said.

Only if mysterious is a synonym for crazy! After dinner, as she was washing the dishes, I slid in behind her to fulfill her wishes, only to find out that her question about groping was *not* an invitation to grope. Messy and unpredictable!

Laura here, chiming in on the arousal bit. Men are visually stimulated, and very easily I might add. Ladies, we need to understand this. Jay says, "Laura, if you're breathing, I'm aroused!"

He's joking of course, but there is a bit of truth there. I can remember very early in our marriage, we struggled in this area. Jay was constantly looking for ways to help me understand what a great need he had for sex.

One day he said to me, "Laura, sex is like the air I breathe."

"Honey," I replied, "we better find you some oxygen tanks!"

I, too, was joking, but there was also some truth in what I was trying to say. I did not need or desire sex on the level that he did. As a young woman, I did not understand this man I had married, or his sexual drive. As I have gotten older—and we have grown in our marriage—I have come to realize that men connect with their wives through sexual intimacy. They are not pigs for desiring sex. They are men who love their wives and want to connect with her the way God intended. Yes, it is messy and unpredictable, but learning your spouse's sexual needs goes a long way to eliminating frustration in the bedroom.

Openly Discuss your Sex Life

The key to any and all parts of any relationship is good communication. Even more so for a marriage. Communication in
marriage is a connecting point. There is a difference between
communication and conversation. Back to my handy dandy
thesaurus! Conversation is *to chat, to discuss, an exchange of
words.* Communication means *to connect, interact, reveal, to
give to another.* Communication can be—but it is not always—
an exchange of words.

We communicate verbally as well as non-verbally. Our body
language, our facial expressions, as well as the act of making
love, are all communication. Conversation is a part of that, and
it is an especially important part for women.

Communicating openly about your sex life involves conversation, specifically open and frank discussions. As with anything
in life, we cannot expect another person to "just know" what
we are thinking and/or feeling. It is unfair to expect your
spouse to know what you need from them, if you haven't told
them. Whether it is in the bedroom or any other area, they
don't just know.

Ladies, we are the worst at this! We expect our husbands to
have mastered Mind Reading 101. Men are not mind-readers.
They do not get subtle hints or innuendo. Your husband needs
to be educated about what you need from him. If it involves
taking out the trash, then ask him to take out the trash. Don't
just tell him that the trash is full and expect that he will make
the leap to knowing that you want the trash taken out. Neither
can you expect him to know what you like and dislike in the
bedroom. He is a man. He likes it all, and will assume you do
too, unless you tell him otherwise.

Gentlemen, on the flip side, you cannot expect your wife to understand the connection you feel with her when you make love, unless you communicate this to her. Case in point: the oxygen tanks I thought Jay needed to purchase earlier in our marriage. Tell her that once a month is not enough for you. Unless, of course, it is.

The 20% is Normal, Too

We all assume that men think about sex more than women. It turns out that this is not always true. In about 20% of marriages, the wife actually has the higher sex drive. If your marriage falls in that 20%, discussing this with your spouse is crucial to your relationship. Men, if you're not open with your wife about this, she will assume there is something wrong *with her*.

Our culture communicates through television, movies, and music that all men are sex-crazed beings. She's noticed you don't desire her like culture says you will. She cannot figure out why. She comes to the conclusion that the problem must lie with her. She will think she is no longer attractive to you, that she is not interesting enough to pursue, or that you are getting your satisfaction elsewhere. Be transparent and have this conversation with her. It will help her to understand you and herself in a new way.

If you cannot communicate—or have a conversation—over a cup of coffee, you will not be able to communicate—or make love—in the bedroom! Sexuality is messy and unpredictable, but openly discussing your sex life helps in so many ways.

Vow to Meet your Spouse's Needs

Can we all admit we are selfish people? From the moment we are born, we want what we want and we will kick, scream and cry until we get it. The selfishness we were born with hasn't changed just because we are adults, it just looks different. We still want what we want and we want it now. Marriage just has a way of shining a spotlight on that selfishness.

In this particular chapter we are discussing sexually submitting to each other to make the most of the sexual mess in marriage. A synonym for submission is *surrender*. Surrender is the giving up of oneself. It is laying aside what I want, when I want it, for the sake of the marriage.

> *"Submit to one another out of reverence for Christ.*
> *Wives, submit yourselves to your own husbands as you*
> *do to the Lord. For the husband is the head of the wife*
> *as Christ is the head of the church, his body, of which*
> *he is the Savior. Now as the church submits to Christ,*
> *so also wives should submit to their husbands in*
> *everything. Husbands love your wives, just as Christ*
> *loved the church and gave himself up for her."*
> *–Ephesians 5:21-25*

We are surrendering to one another as a form of worship. "Out of reverence for Christ" in the above passage means worship. We have surrendered our lives to Jesus; in that same way we surrender to each other. Ladies, we surrender to our husbands not in a throw-in-the-towel mindset, but rather in an act of yielding in humility. Gentlemen, your act of surrender is in loving your wife the way Jesus loves us—by giving Himself in sacrifice.

I know what you're thinking. Laura, I don't have time to think of his needs! Do you know how many other things I have to worry about in a day? What am I packing the kids for lunch today? Where do the kids have to be today after school and at what time? The laundry is piling up, when am I going to get that done? What time is the meeting about the new project at work? I need to schedule interviews for 2 new employees. I need to let the pastor know I cannot make it to the church event tomorrow. I need to schedule doctor appointments for wellness check ups. When do I have time this week to pick up groceries? I hope he's not expecting a home-made dinner tonight!

Girl, I feel your pain. I have been there. I am still there on a regular basis. At times it's as if we just need a few more hours in a day to get everything done. However, when we try to do everything, we end up putting our husbands at the end of the line. He is an adult, he can take care of himself. He doesn't need me like the kids do.

Yes he does. The need just looks different. The best thing we can do for our kids is to love our husband—*first*. We have to surrender our need to take care of everyone else and make him our top priority.

Jay here. Scripture is meant to be lived out between husband and wife first before it can be lived out any place else. To sexually submit to one another out of reverence for Christ is a tough thing to do. Guys, I am writing specifically to you for just a second. My father always taught me "ladies first", and he wasn't just talking about holding the door open. It is a principle that also applies to your sex life. Most of us are selfish in the bedroom. Most of us don't know how to be great lovers. Ladies, you can help us with that by clearly and unapologetically communicating your needs. But, Gentlemen, you need to think about your wife's needs both in the bedroom and beyond. For her all is right in the bedroom when all is right in her world. Strive to make "all right" in her world, and you'll be well on your way to meeting her sexual needs.

Here's a little tip: meeting each other's needs *will involve planning*. If you don't plan for it, it isn't going to happen. Life will creep in and take over. It might sound too methodical to be romantic, but believe me, spontaneity is overrated. Plan and schedule your intimate times. That doesn't mean that your time will be less than romantic or fun. Actually, when you plan ahead, the anticipation makes the time way better than if it were to happen spur-of-the-moment!

Enjoy the Gift

A huge part of making the most of our sexual mess is learning to enjoy the gift that God created. It's that simple! The nature of a gift is that it is free. It doesn't come with strings or conditions. It is meant simply to be received and enjoyed.

Gifts are really important to Laura. Every Christmas, I pride myself on surprising her with a gift she has not even thought about. The delight in her eyes and the squeal when she opens the gift fills me with joy.

God created sex for husband and wife to enjoy. It is not supposed to be an obligation or a chore. Rather, it is a beautiful gift, beautifully packaged for us to unwrap together. I imagine God looking down on a husband and wife enjoying His gift, smiling and saying, "Yep, I gave that to you! Enjoy my children, enjoy!"

Your Reflections

Ask your spouse this question: Which of the areas of learning to **L-O-V-E,** outlined in this chapter, do I need to work on? Listen carefully to their response and choose one thing you can do this week to start meeting their needs.

_____

_____

_____

_____

_____

_____

_____

_____

_____

_____

_____

Chapter 8

We're all a Mess Spiritually

The Bible tells us that we have all sinned and fallen short of the glory of God. Let me translate that for you. We've all screwed up, and we're all a mess spiritually. If we were to be completely honest, this is the root of the mess in every other area of life. I (Jay) figured that after over 50 years of life that I'd have this whole walk with God thing worked out. I don't. I'm still human, and I still make messes—some worse than others.

Even Over Prayer

Laura with you here. When our kids were young, we started a habit of taking time to pray with them. Before they left for school everyday, we would gather in the living room and pray for their safety, for any tests they had coming up, for friendship and whatever else might be on their minds. We would end each prayer time with our hands in the middle of the circle and yell, "Go Jesus!" We prayed at every meal, not only for our food, but also for whatever concerns had arisen during the day. We prayed with them every night before they went to sleep. Jay and I would pray for them many times during the day as well, whenever they would come to mind.

When they left the nest, we let that habit slide. They were now responsible for themselves. Our job was done, and we were determined to enjoy this new season of life. We still talked and texted them regularly, but our habit of praying for them every day slipped to the back of our minds. Recently were convicted that we should continue to pray for them daily.

Now, we text them all at the beginning of the week and ask for any specific prayer requests they may have. Then, we set an alarm on Jay's phone for 2:26pm everyday as our reminder to pray.

Why 2:26pm? Because we are believing in the words of Proverbs:

"Train up a child in the way he should go, even when he is old he will not depart from it." –Proverbs 22:6

Everyday, Jay's alarm on his phone dings at 2:26. No matter where we are, we pray out loud for our kids. It may be in the grocery store, walking the streets of Chicago, in the TSA line of the Detroit Airport—where ever we are. When the alarm sounds, one of us will say, "I will pray," and we take turns.

Here's the messed up part: recently, we were both diligently working on this manuscript. Jay was at the counter and I was in front of the fireplace in my favorite chair. The alarm rang. I was in the zone. I couldn't be interrupted. Instead of saying "I will pray," I said, "Your turn."

Jay replied, "I prayed for lunch. It is your turn."

"Well I prayed for the kids yesterday. It is your turn," I shot back.

"And I prayed for them the day before!"

"Exactly! So it is your turn!" I replied, drilling him with a stare. I knew I was right.

After a moment of tension, we both stopped and laughed. We were arguing over who would pray for our kids. That's messed up!

We've Stepped in It

Our conference at Grand Hotel on Mackinac Island is unique for a number of reasons. First, Grand Hotel is not just a hotel. It's an experience. Second, it fits our style for our conferences, which is learning through fun rather than lecture. The third reason we love it is because Mackinac Island is truly one of a kind. They do not allow cars anywhere on the island. Transportation is by horse drawn carriage.

An interesting fact about horses is that they poop. And sometimes, especially while wandering around the island, you step in it. If you spend enough time around horses, it's eventually going to happen. In the time we've spent on Mackinac, we've had the privilege of seeing a number of different levels of "stepping in it" that just happen to correspond perfectly with married life!

1) You just get a little on the bottom of your shoe and you can pretty much rub it off on the grass. These are issues like speaking to your spouse in a poor tone of voice or failing to keep your word. Inappropriate, but not really a threat to your marriage. A sincere apology will usually clean up this mess.

2) You have really stepped in it and it's all over your shoes. You're going to have to wash it off before moving forward. In marriage it can be something like hurtful words, or withhold-

ing affection or sex. You need to admit you have done something wrong and make amends with your spouse.

3) Not only did you step in it; you slipped, you fell on it, and you rolled around in it. Affairs, pornography, and credit card debt are examples. These are issues that can devastate a marriage. To move forward you need to seek help to restore your marriage.

Nobody plans to "step in it" when it comes to marriage, but there is a war waging in the heart and soul of every one of us: our sin nature. While forgiven by the grace of God, it is still present within us. Even the Apostle Paul wrote in Romans 7:15-20:

"I do not understand what I do. For what I want to do I do not do, but what I hate I do. 16 And if I do what I do not want to do, I agree that the law is good. 17 As it is, it is no longer I myself who do it, but it is sin living in me. 18 For I know that good itself does not dwell in me, that is, in my sinful nature. For I have the desire to do what is good, but I cannot carry it out. 19 For I do not do the good I want to do, but the evil I do not want to do—this I keep on doing. 20 Now if I do what I do not want to do, it is no longer I who do it, but it is sin living in me that does it."

Your Sin Nature is Showing

In a quiet forest ran a gentle stream. Many animals would come each day to drink of the pure clean water. On the sunny side of the stream lived a turtle, and on the shady bank lived a scorpion.

Everyday the scorpion would watch the turtle with envy as he sunned himself or took a refreshing swim in the gently flowing stream. The scorpion longed to feel the sun but found no way to cross the stream. Not even in late summer, when the stream was just a trickle, could the scorpion find rocks to scurry across.

One beautiful summer day, the turtle was swimming in the clear water. The scorpion shuffled out on the furthest rock.

"Mr. Turtle, I have a proposal for you. Would you be so kind as to float up to my rock, let me crawl on your back, and swim me to the sunny side? I've never been there and I long to do so. I won't sting you because I can't swim. If I did, we'd both die."

Mr. Turtle replied, "Let me think on it overnight and I'll give you my answer tomorrow."

The kind turtle thought long and hard through the night about the scorpions proposal. He ran through every scenario and always came to the conclusion that there would be no way the scorpion would sting him, as it would mean certain death for the scorpion.

The next day, Mr. Turtle agreed and pulled up next to the rock where the scorpion had been waiting. The scorpion climbed on and away they went. Halfway across the stream the scorpion crawled near the front of the turtle and, with all his might, drove his stinger into the neck of the turtle. The turtle looked back at the scorpion, shocked and surprised as he felt his own life slipping away from the power of the venom.

"But why?" he asked, "Now both of us will die."

"I'm a scorpion," the scorpion replied. "It's in my nature to sting."

And with that they both perished.

None of us stand at the altar planning how we will mess our marriage up, but between the wiley ways of Satan and our sin nature, we do things that make a mess and make our own lives miserable. Life has a way of bringing out our sin nature, whether we mean it to or not.

This isn't Fair!

Brooke here. There are few life experiences that will show you your sin nature more clearly than parenting. I think God designed it that way on purpose to bring everything in us that isn't of him to the surface. Nothing brings out my impatience, my short temper and my self-righteousness faster than encountering the sin nature in my own child. It's ugly. It's messy. I don't like admitting that stuff is in there.

While I was growing up, Dr. James Dobson was the expert on parenting. He was known for saying, "Parenting isn't for cowards." Well, that is true. Why is parenting not for cowards, you ask? Because *parenting isn't fair*. I know this. I am regularly victimized by a human half my size, and I'm supposed to put up with it with love and grace and intentionality.

Recently, while brushing her teeth, my daughter wanted to pull her sleeves up. Being unsuccessful at first, she immediately lost her temper with me as if I should have long ago anticipated her needs.

"Mommy can you PLEASE pull my sleeves up!" came the angry cry, full of frustration. I am used to this, since these outbursts are a daily occurrence at this stage. I responded calmly, as I am training myself to do. With a few words of encouragement, she was able to raise the sleeve to her satisfaction.

Without thinking, I reached to help her with the second sleeve, which—much to my surprise—she did not appreciate.

"I DON'T NEED HELP!" she screamed at me.

Righteous indignation rose from my chest up to my eyeballs. I might have tried to call fire down from heaven except that I was so shocked by what had just happened, I stood there staring at her, dumbfounded. *Lord of mercy, do you see how this child you gave me treats me? This is just not fair!*

There's a lot we deal with in family relationships that just isn't fair. Life isn't fair. The only sure thing is that we will not be treated fairly all the time. As imperfect human beings living with other imperfect human beings, we are going to step on each other and get stepped on once in a while. It is a sign of maturity to give grace in those moments, instead of demanding fairness. That means I have to give grace to my toddler in those moments when she's pushing all my buttons at once and my own tendency to demand respect wants to take over. Oops. My sin nature is showing again.

This also applies to marriage. We must also respond to our spouses with grace, love and patience. Yes, even when we are not being treated fairly. Jesus modeled this for us when He remained silent before His accusers; when He allowed Himself to be brutally beaten, mocked, and even crucified. Was that fair? Of course not. Jesus is the ultimate example of responding with love and grace, even when He wasn't deserving of any of it. He did that to show us that we can, too. We must resist our sin nature, and follow Jesus' example.

How do we resist both our sin nature and the Devil who wants nothing more than to cause us pain and suffering in our marriages? There is only one way; to seek the grace of Jesus daily and call on the power of the Holy Spirit. Satan flees when confronted with the power of the Holy Spirit. As scripture says,

"Submit yourselves, then, to God. Resist the devil, and he will flee from you." –James 4:7

Don't Waste the Power

The story is told of a wealthy woman who owned a castle in England. She was approached by the newly formed electric company asking if she'd like to be the first castle in England to have electricity. She knew being the first would bring her great prestige, so she agreed.

The company not only ran a line to her house but set up lights in every room. They, too, were aware of the prestige they would receive from being the first to electrify one of the great houses. They were also driven by the income her electric use would bring.

After a few months, the electric company noticed that the lady was not using much power. In fact, she was using hardly any at all. They dispatched the salesman who sold her on the idea to see what was going on.

She welcomed him into the castle and talked about how much she liked having electricity. It made her life so much easier. When asked why she uses so little power she responded that she only leaves the lights on long enough to light her candles and oil lamps.

"All this power and you choose to light your room with a candle? It seems senseless," the salesman responded.

The same can be true in our marriages when we rely on our friends advice, or the latest TV guru instead of tapping into the power of the Holy Spirit. We are all a mess spiritually. We have all fallen short. We have all tried to go on our own power, forgetting that the Holy Spirit is available to us. We have all stepped in it, and we've all got mess on us. The good news is that we can make the most of this mess.

Your Reflections

What areas of your marriage are you still operating on "candle power" instead of letting the Holy Spirit take over?

_____

_____

_____

_____

_____

_____

_____

_____

_____

Chapter 9

Spiritually Surrender

The action we have to take in this spiritual mess is to spiritually surrender. Let's look at Ephesians 6:12:

"For our struggle is not against flesh and blood, but against the rulers, against the authorities, against the powers of this dark world and against the spiritual forces of evil in the heavenly realms."

Here's the reality folks. Your spouse is not the person you are fighting against. He or she is not your enemy. The passage above from Ephesians tells us who our enemy is. It's a spiritual force, because it's a spiritual battle. If you call yourself a Christian, you are in a battle against spiritual forces of evil. The enemy is going to try to destroy your marriage.

We see it in our culture every day. We see it in the news. We see it everywhere we turn. Marriage does not hold the same virtue or importance that it used to hold years ago. Marriage is under attack. This is not a political statement, but truth. Realize that when you are disagreeing, when you feel your marriage is in shambles, and things aren't the way they are supposed to be, your spouse is not the enemy.

A phrase we say to each other almost daily is, "I am your biggest fan." I'm your biggest fan. I'm not your enemy. I'm your partner. I'm your teammate. The fight we fight is not against each other, but against a spiritual force, and in case you didn't know already, it's a battle that has been won for us!

When you're feeling like a mess, whether it be mentally, emotionally, sexually, or spiritually, practice mentally melding, emotionally exercising self-control, sexually submitting and *spiritually surrendering*.

The Strength in Submission

Place your hands together with your fingertips touching. Now, bow your middle fingers between your palms until your knuckles touch. Your middle fingers represent you and your spouse in humble submission to one another.

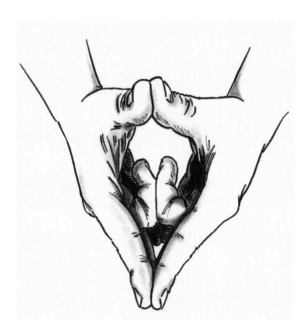

It should be pretty easy to separate your thumbs without moving any other fingers. They represent your parents—that we were meant to grow up and spiritually separate ourselves from them. Your index fingers represent your siblings. They are also easy to separate. Your pinky fingers are your children, which will also one day be independent from you.

Your ring finger, however is a different story. If you haven't already, go ahead and try to separate your ring fingers. These represent your marriage. With your middle fingers bent toward each other, it is impossible to pull those two fingers apart. In a similar fashion, while you two are humbly submitted to one another it is impossible for your marriage to break apart. One key to staying happily married is to walk a life of submission.

I (Jay) can admit I'm a first-born, type A personality who likes to be in charge. I can be a bit of a control freak. When I met Laura, one of the things that attracted me most was her easy-going, laid back lifestyle. She would always let me take the lead. One of the problems I deal with is that I can bulldoze right over people and not even know it. I get so focused on what I want, it blinds me.

The person I've bulldozed more than any is Laura, and I'm not proud of it. Early in our marriage my mind set was that I know what I want and I know where I'm going. Anything Laura thought or said was inconsequential. The problem was that my take charge attitude had me squelching many of the gifts God had given Laura.

I vividly remember when the Lord showed me the error of my ways. It was 2004 at a Celebrate Your Marriage Conference on Mackinac Island. We had been married 20 years, we had been doing the conferences for 8 years, and we had created a partnership with WUGN Family Life Radio to promote the event for the past 4 years.

We stepped off the stage at the conclusion of the conference and were immediately greeted by Peter and Lynette Brooks. Peter was the station manager and morning show host for WUGN and had attended the conference as part of our agreement.

Peter spoke first. "Hey, we wanted to let you know this is our 4th time at the conference and this was by far the best one yet!" Lynette was standing next to him, poking him in the side.

"Why, thank you!" I replied, "That means a lot coming from you two."

There was an awkward silence. Lynette was still poking Peter in the ribs.

Peter broke the silence. "Would you like to know why?"

"For sure."

He looked straight at me. "It's because you shut up and let Laura talk!" His index finger was pointing straight at my bride.

Peter and Lynette both started to laugh. After a quick moment of reflection I laughed too, but their message hit home. Laura had valuable insight that I was robbing from our listeners.

For the 8 years we'd been doing Celebrate Your Marriage Conferences, I frequently stepped on Laura when she would speak. I'd interrupt her, correct her, or just take over for her in front of hundreds of people. I was totally humiliating her. When she'd tell me after the event, I'd shrug it off thinking she didn't know what she was talking about. This message from our friends, Peter and Lynette, really hit home. I had not submitted to her abilities when it came to making presentations.

Unbeknownst to me, Laura had made her own plans to put me in my place. She had our sound technician, Bill, hide a roll of gaff tape near her stage monitor. Gaff tape is thick and wide and very sticky. It's made to tape down cords on carpet so people don't trip. The first time I cut her off, she was going to get out the gaff tape and put it over my mouth! It would have been hilarious, but for the first time in 8 years, I didn't once step on her.

Submission Goes Both Ways

"Submit to one another out of reverence for Christ."
—Ephesians 5:21

Thankfully I've learned the areas where Laura shines, and now practice submission to the best of my ability. For example: decorating our house. If I insisted that I decorate the house, I'd paint everything beige. By submitting to Laura's giftedness in this area, our house looks like it came out of an HGTV special!

We love what we do. We travel the country encouraging couples to celebrate marriage using music, comedy and Biblical truth. The hardest part of our job is travel. Airplanes, rental cars, hotels all make it a challenge to get good rest, exercise and proper nutrition. As a result we've had to create some very disciplined habits. For example:

- I drive; Laura navigates (with her iPhone of course).
- I book the airline tickets, but Laura handles keeping the luggage claim tickets in order.
- We split meals at restaurants.
- We have our own specific tasks when we enter a hotel room for the first time.
- I take care of the luggage; Laura plugs in all the devices.
- I take the luggage cart back to the lobby; Laura distributes the bags to the appropriate places.
- I get ice for the room; Laura puts away any food in the refrigerator.

We have a system that works for us. One time recently, as we entered our hotel room for the first time in a new place, Laura started barking orders at me like I used to do to her. I stopped what I was doing and turned to her.

"There's only room for ONE Jay in this marriage."

Then we both laughed!

A Note to the Women from Laura

I want to disassociate submission with passivity. Submission is in no way passive. Submission is an active choice that we must make. The idea of wives submitting to their husbands is for *order*—as in the opposite of chaos, not hierarchy.

Imagine a man and a woman dancing an intricate dance. This is not a modern dance where two people just take the floor and do their own thing, but the kind of dancing where two partners are performing in complete unison with one another. It takes a lot of practice to reach that level of perfection. It also takes order: a specific leader and a specific follower. The leader is not the most important part here. The follower is equally important in making the dance perfectly smooth and beautiful.

In marriage, there must be a leader and a follower. It won't be the man in every case, just because he's the man. In many areas, the wife is the more capable leader. However, in order to make a marriage flow like a perfectly choreographed movement, one will have to lead and one will have to follow. This flow is best achieved when we submit to each other, recognizing the skills and gifts that God has placed in each partner.

For those that insist that God instituted and anointed the man of the household as its spiritual leader—and therefore the man is over the wife—you're right. He did. He also made him *responsible* and *accountable* for it. What a burden to carry! Men, don't be too quick to claim authority over your wife without also shouldering the responsibility that you have before God to love her, nurture her, provide for her, make wise decisions for your family, and *submit to the Holy Spirit*. Before you use scripture to demand submission of your wife, check your own heart. Are you leading the way by submitting yourself wholly to Christ? Your authority over your family is only as strong as God's authority over your own life. Humbly practice submission to Christ, which includes honoring and submitting to the Holy Spirit moving in and speaking through your spouse.

A Cord of Three Strands

I (Jay) used to speak at a lot of youth camps and, to this day, Laura and I speak at a lot of family camps. We love it!

At these camps there will usually be a field day where all sorts of games and activities take place for the entire family. It's like family Olympics. One of my favorites is the three-legged race. Two people stand side by side and have their middle ankles tied together, so they essentially have three legs between the two of them. Then they must race to the end of the field. The first pair to reach the finish line wins.

3-2-1 GO! The fun begins as the pairs try to coordinate their three legs to function together. My favorite is to watch a 6-foot-tall dad trying to run with his 4-foot-tall kid. Eventually, dad just picks him up and runs with him. The ones who win usually start off slowly and establish a rhythm, then they gradually build that rhythm into speed.

Marriage can often feel like a three-legged race where we just can't seem to get our rhythm right. It is hard to coordinate three legs, especially when one of them is not attached to your body. But the extra strength you have together becomes an asset when you are moving in rhythm. The number 3 has huge significance in the Bible:

112

- Father, Son & Holy Spirit
- Abraham, Isaac & Jacob
- Shadrach, Meshach & Abednego
- Peter, James & John
- Larry, Curly & Moe

That last one might not be in the Bible now that I think about it.

Ecclesiastes states a very important fact about 3's:

> "Though one may be overpowered, two can defend t hemselves. A cord of three strands is not easily broken."
> —Ecclesiastes 4:12

This is such a strong statement when it comes to marriage. If only one of you is fighting for your marriage to survive, you can be overpowered easily by the forces at work in our world today. If the two of you are fighting together you can defend your marriage better. However, when we invite God to play an active role in our marriage we will not easily be broken.

Just what does being a "cord of three strands" look like? Is it that we go to church every week and serve when we can? No, but that is a very good thing to do. Is it that we pray before meals? No, but again, it's a good thing to do. What about doing devotions together? By now you know where this is going. It's good, but it alone is not the key.

Picture your marriage as a triangle with Christ at the top and you and your spouse at the other two points of the triangle.

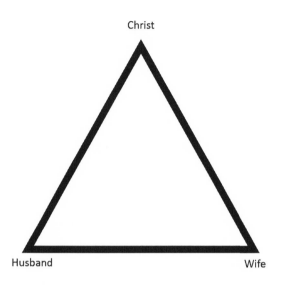

Christ

Husband   Wife

Becoming part of a church, serving the body, participating in public prayer and disciplining yourself in regular devotions are all good for your spiritual development, but first and foremost, your heart must be set on becoming like Christ. Remember, in James we read that the prayer of a righteous person is powerful and effective. This is your act of spiritual surrender to the Lord. You both must pray this prayer for yourselves: "God, through the power of Your Holy Spirit make me more like Jesus today."

Look at the triangle again. If both husband and wife commit to pray daily to draw closer to Christ, what's going to happen to their relationship? They will also draw closer together. That's the power of spiritual surrender. When I become more like Christ, I become exactly what Laura needs in a husband. And when Laura becomes more like Christ, she becomes exactly what I need in a wife. The same holds true in your marriage.

Your Reflections

What steps can you take today to draw closer to Jesus?

_____

_____

_____

_____

_____

_____

_____

_____

_____

_____

_____

_____

_____

Part Two

Chapter 10

Live FREE

There's a Christian group from our hometown of Alma, Michigan called Sidewalk Prophets. They put on a free concert this summer in Alma and a group of us went to hear them. There was a bunch of little kids at this concert. It was amazing to watch them freely express themselves in worship. Kids are so full of joy, untainted by the struggles of a difficult life. It is no wonder that Jesus used these little children as an example for us. We were created to live free and alive, with the faith of a little child, but how is that possible in the midst of a messy marriage? How can we be free and live with joy and abandon when we're not ok?

It is Ok that We're not Ok

We're not ok and you're not ok, and that's ok. I (Jay) am going to share with you why that's ok. I'm going to sum up the whole Bible—from Genesis to the maps—in one page.

In the beginning, God created. Stop there. The first thing that happened in scripture was God created. This is important. God is creative, and when he created you he made you creative too. Creation is always a messy process. It takes a lot of mess to create the most beautiful, intricate masterpiece. In fact, you can argue that the more detailed the piece, the more mess must be created in the process. Creativity is part of us. So is the mess that follows.

God spoke the universe into existence. This is how big God is.

He didn't have to make anything with his hands. He spoke and there was light. He spoke and there was the earth and the sea. He spoke and there were birds in the sky and fish in the water. He spoke and there were animals and grasses and all sorts of things.

After each creation, He said "It is good." He made the earth and the sea, and He said, "That's good." He made the sun and the stars, and He said, "That's good." He made the zebra, the

120

giraffe, the duck billed platypus, and He said, "Strange, but good."

Then God did something different. He didn't speak this next being. He reached down and formed this being from the dust of the earth. Instead of *speaking* life into this being, He *breathed* life. He created man.
God created man for one reason and one reason only. To have

a relationship with him. That's why God created each and every one of us. The God who spoke the universe into being wants to have a relationship with us. That is really cool.

You know the really amazing thing? When God made man, He did not say that it was good. When God made man, He said that it was *very good*. You may not agree. You may look in the mirror and say, "not good". We battle our past, decisions we've made, or decisions we didn't make. We don't often like ourselves. We all have baggage, but God made you in His image, and He says you are very good.

The problem is sin. When Adam and Eve brought sin into the world, it stepped between God and man. It's that simple. The bible tells us this about God. He is so holy He cannot even look on sin. The Bible tells us that sin takes us in the complete opposite direction of God. Wrap your head around this. If God is forever going in one direction and sin is taking us forever the opposite way, that's hell. To go further and further from God, that's hell. This is the problem we face. And this, my friends, is why we're not ok.

The Center

Laura and I spend some time counseling other couples on occasion. I was counseling a young man a couple weeks ago. He began by giving me a list of all the things that are wrong with his wife. The truth is, the things he listed are not the problem. They are symptoms of the problem. I told him the real problem is that God is not the center of his marriage.

This is the root cause of marital problems. We've already established that you and your spouse are two very different human beings. There is no way that two humans that are planets apart can get on the same page and act of one accord without God holding such a union together. He must form the center of your marriage if it is to be successful.

I'm not saying that it is easy or that we get it right all the time. We don't wake up singing a praise song and then our day goes perfect. Our marriage is messy, and many days we're just not ok. But that is ok, because there was one perfect man who lived a perfect life, and died so that we could receive His reward, instead of our own.

God sent Jesus to the earth. All that God is—all the power that spoke the universe into existence—was shrunk down into the form of a baby. A human baby. Then He grew up and lived a perfect life. He came and did all that we could not do for ourselves. There is no other being in heaven or on earth who could—or would—do that for us.

The skeptics out there may doubt. What about Buddha? What about Muhammed? How do we coexist peacefully with other religions who say we are wrong? I think God is ok with our questions, but there is something bigger worth noting here. Buddha and Muhammed never claimed to be God.

In every major religion practiced in the world today, the leader never said that he was God, except for one. That one was Jesus Christ. Jesus walked the earth and He said, "I'm God." He claimed to be God incarnate, God in the flesh. He proved it when they crucified Him and He did not stay dead. He rose from the grave.

How do you know that? Where is the proof? How do we know for sure that the account of Christ is really accurate and not just made up by his followers?

More people saw Jesus Christ alive after He was crucified than saw Abraham Lincoln get shot. Abraham Lincoln getting shot is a historical fact. People seeing him dead is a historical fact. Jesus Christ being crucified, dead and buried is also a historical fact. People wrote it down. Historians like Josephus wrote this down. More than 500 people testified that they saw Jesus alive after He was dead.

You Can Live F-R-E-E

What happened when Jesus lived a perfect life, died, was buried and rose again? He completely covered sin. In fact, He separated sin as far as the east is from the west. He did it for one reason. He did it so that God and Man could once again be friends. Because of the restoration He provided between us and Him, we can also have restoration between husband and wife. We are not ok and you are not ok, but because of what Jesus did, it's ok.

You may have noticed we love acronyms. It helps us remember things. We want to give you four steps that will help you begin to experience freedom in the midst of your messy marriage. They just happen to spell the word *free*.

F—forgive
R—restore
E—engage
E—experience

Forgive

We love partnering with Thrivent Financial because 1) they are a Christ centered financial services company and 2) whether you have lots or you have none, money is an issue in every marriage. Early in our relationship it certainly was an issue for us.

Laura was never really taught to budget or make money work for her instead of her working for her money. When we met she had a really good job. Laura secured the job right after college graduation, and she lived with her mom so she didn't have many living expenses. Still, in six weeks time she managed to bounce 14 checks!

That's when we met. She was a financial disaster, and as soon as she said yes to my marriage proposal, we combined our checkbooks into one account. I took over running the books and had our finances squared away within weeks.

As we walked through married life together, I began to teach Laura about budgeting, how to tithe and save. I'll never forget the first time I had her write a tithe check to the church. We were both making about fifteen hundred dollars each month ($3,000.00 total) so I told her to write a check to the church for three hundred dollars.

She stopped with an astounded look on her face.

"You mean thirty dollars, right?"

"No," I said, "three hundred dollars. One-tenth of three thousand is three hundred."

"But three hundred dollars would buy us a washing machine and we don't have one yet."

"We're going to do this right from the beginning and the Lord will take care of the rest."

Over the next eight years we did the books together and Laura was beginning to see that a budget is actually freeing! Right after our son was born, she announced to me that she thought she could do the books on her own. I was getting busy speaking at youth events, so I thought it was a good idea.

For the next two years, every time I'd speak at a camp or

conference, I'd ask for two checks. One for my honorarium and one for my travel expenses. I deposited the travel expense checks into a secret account I set up to save money for a fun 10th anniversary celebration.

During those two years I saved up two thousand dollars. To a couple of youth ministers in 1994, that seemed like a million bucks! My plan was to have a romantic dinner at home and then have her open an envelope stuffed with travel brochures and 20 one hundred dollar bills.

My plan worked perfectly. Dinner was fantastic, we cleaned up and we sat back down at the dining room table. I handed her the envelope.

"Happy 10th anniversary!" I said.

She spread everything out in front of her and her eyes welled up in tears.

I thought I must have really outdone myself. A split second later her tears turned to gut wrenching sobs. I was totally confused. She was crying like I'd never seen her cry before. After she finally calmed down, she told be what was making her so emotional.

"I've been trying to work up the courage to tell you I'm not ready to take over the books. The $2,000.00 sitting in front of me is exactly how much credit card debt I've built up without you knowing."

I just sat there holding her, stunned. I didn't know what to say. She broke the silence.

"I can't believe I've ruined everything, I'm so sorry."

127

"You're forgiven and you haven't ruined everything," I replied. "We have a debt and we have the money to pay off that debt. We can plan a trip another time."

We took the money, put it in our checking account and paid off the credit card the next day. It felt fantastic!

I could have reacted very differently. Honestly there have been other times I wasn't so quick to forgive. I could have screamed and yelled and called her names, but I chose forgiveness. You see that is why forgiveness is so powerful? It's a *choice* we make. When we choose forgiveness, it is truly *freeing*.

> *"Bear with each other and forgive one another...*
> *forgive as the Lord forgave you."*
> *– Col.3:13*

Restore

It would have been very easy for me to tell Laura she was no longer doing the books, but that wouldn't have benefitted either Laura, myself or our marriage.

Ongoing forgiveness is required if we are going to restore trust that has been broken. Our relationship with God is a perfect example of ongoing forgiveness. Jesus forgave my sins of the past. He forgives me today, and will likewise forgive my future sins.

When it came to Laura's financial debacle, I had to forgive her almost on a daily basis for the first couple of weeks. When she'd call herself stupid or dumb for running up the credit card, I'd reassure her that in fact she was not stupid or dumb.

She simply made a costly mistake.

I had to continually remind her that she will learn from this experience and that ultimately she'd walk away with a better understanding of how to deal with money. Slowly she began to feel confident we could do the books together again.

Engage

If I were going to help Laura find freedom in doing the finances, I was going to have to actively engage with her. So the first thing we did was to review the family budget. We had clearly lined out what our fixed expenses were and how much should be left over at the end of the month. Our model was, and still is, the 10-10-10-70 principle.

10% goes to the Lord
10% goes to long term retirement savings
10% goes to the emergency fund*
70% goes to pay our bills

*When the emergency fund reaches an agreed upon amount, that 10% becomes fun money until the emergency fund dips below set amount. It then goes to replenish that fund until it's full again.

After reviewing the budget, Laura and I would sit down twice a month and pay the bills together. When we had an emergency, like a storm knocking down several large trees near the house, we used the emergency fund to cover their removal. Thankfully we had more than enough money in the emergency fund, and actually received a discount for paying cash.
I was able to show Laura a perfect example of our money

working for us—a discount for paying cash—as opposed to us working for our money—interest on a credit card bill.

Experience

Slowly over the next couple years I backed away from the books. We now just review the finances every quarter. Laura has mastered the art of budgeting and will even say to me from time to time, "That purchase will have to wait until next month."

Living F-R-E-E (as well as forming a good family budget) is a key way to experiencing the most of this messy marriage. Fast forward to our 25th anniversary, Laura had saved up enough money for us to take a cruise around the islands of Hawaii. We had the time of our lives and even learned how to surf. Well, Laura learned how to surf. I learned 600 ways to fall off a surfboard. She's now working on an Italy fund for our 40th. Thankfully she still has a few years to make that happen.

In the next few chapters, we will take an in depth look at how living F-R-E-E can apply to your marriage.

Your Reflections

_____

_____

_____

_____

Chapter 11

Forgive

The first step in living F-R-E-E is to forgive. Forgiveness is available to us because of what Jesus did.

A really good friend of ours, Ron Deal, has a ministry to blended families. He has lots of great things to share about marriage, especially blended marriages. One quote of his I love to share says, "Marriage will always require more of you than you anticipate." Just let that sink in.

Aside from everything else marriage requires of you, you have to go and forgive your spouse after they really step in it, make a mess, hurt your feelings or offend you. That's a really hard part of marriage. Good thing the example has already been set for us. We have been forgiven by God.

C.S. Lewis once said, "To be a Christian means to forgive the inexcusable, because God has forgiven the inexcusable in you." Ouch. Since we have been forgiven in such a world-shifting, life-altering way, we also have to forgive.

Sometimes it's not our spouse who we must forgive, but ourselves. This is even more difficult. I hear all the time, "I know God forgives me but I just can't forgive myself." This is pride, and it's gotta go. If I've done something in my past or to my spouse and I can't forgive myself, I'm saying that I'm more powerful than God—that my decision to hold myself responsible trumps God's decision to forgive me. How arrogant is that?

Tim Keller puts it this way, "When someone says 'I know God forgives me, but I can't forgive myself,' they mean that they have failed an idol, whose approval is more important than God's." That idol is themselves. When we refuse to forgive ourselves completely and fully embrace God's blessing instead of punishment, we are essentially saying we are bigger, stronger, smarter and know better than God.

God has forgiven us. If you have repented, Jesus Christ's blood has covered your sin. You are not more powerful than God, so you better forgive yourself, because he's already forgiven you.

Verbalize and Internalize

Take that C.S. Lewis quote, print it out and hang it on your fridge. Let it sink in how great a thing has been done for us, and how small a thing we are asked to do in return. That's the crux of building a healthy marriage. It's a beautiful expression of God's grace that we are able to offer our spouse.

How do we do this? How do we forgive, practically speaking, when we don't *feel* forgiving?

The first step is to verbalize your forgiveness. Let your mouth—and your decision to forgive—guide your feelings.

Part of verbalizing is learning to speak in a language your spouse understands. You need to learn each other's apology language. My (Jay) love language is words of affirmation. I like to hear love verbally expressed in a way I can understand. So it is important to me to hear the words, "I'm sorry," in a sincere way.

We see how this is lived out in Colossians 3:13:

> *"Bear with each other and forgive one another*
> *if any of you has a grievance against someone.*
> *Forgive as the Lord forgave you."*

One thing Laura and I like to do with scripture is to insert the word "spouse" wherever we can. I read this passage:

> *"Bear with your* spouse *and forgive your* spouse
> *if you have a grievance against them.*
> *Forgive your* spouse *as the Lord forgave you."*

This helps us to verbalize both our repentance and forgiveness. Practice the art of apology and watch your marriage grow.

In our house when someone says I'm sorry, we don't have a choice but to express forgiveness. We believe when there's an apology, there is repentance. Where there is repentance, we must respond with forgiveness.

The second step of forgiveness is to internalize. I want to point out Jesus's words in Luke 23:34. As He was hanging on the cross, having just experienced the greatest physical torture the Roman Empire could devise, He looked down at the people who had beaten him and driven nails into him and those who stood by and watched. Then He said,

> *"Father forgive them for they know not what they do."*

It is incredible that in the midst of such suffering he could forgive them. Why? *Because they know not what they do.*

When your spouse hurts you, so many times they had no idea! Internalizing means dealing with the anger I feel, the bitterness and the hurt. I have to release it and communicate in a calm way with my spouse. It is my responsibility to express lovingly to my spouse when and how she has hurt me.

There are other times when the hurt was intentional. We lose our temper and say something that will provoke a response from our spouse. We jab at places we know are tender. Even when the hurt is intentional, we forgive it.

Let's look at Jesus again. Were the Roman centurions aware of the pain they caused Jesus? Yes. Did they see they were drawing blood? Yes. Did they know that crucifying him would cause his death? Absolutely. They weren't ignorant of their involvement or the result of their actions, but Jesus still said of them, "They do not know..."

Jesus was saying they didn't get it. They didn't see the bigger picture. They didn't understand that they were hanging the son of God on a tree. They didn't understand that an epic battle between good and evil was being waged around them, and even through them.

We don't understand what we are doing in the grand scheme of things when we lash out and hurt each other. Your spouse doesn't see the big picture. Even you don't see the big picture yet. God does, so follow Jesus's example and forgive your spouse. You will reap the benefits if you do.

Forgiveness is Healing

"Therefore confess your sins to one another and pray for each other so that you might be healed." –James 5:16

Confession and forgiveness not only heal your soul but can heal wounds in your relationship. Isn't it odd that the person we love and cherish the most is the one we hurt most often?

Laura hates going over bridges. It scares her to death. She doesn't know why, but it terrifies her. I'll never forget the time we were in Baltimore, MD for an Ultimate Date Night. Baltimore is right on the water, and is full of bridges. We arrived a day early to do some sight seeing, but instead of enjoying the day, Laura spent the day with a death grip on the car door handle.

I, on the other hand, don't mind bridges or heights. I spent the day with my head on a swivel, trying to spot the next ship or cool building.

"You're scaring me to death with the way you're driving over these bridges!" she finally said. She then compared her fear of bridges to my fear of tight spaces. Instantly, I knew just how afraid she really was. My claustrophobia is a real fear for me.

"Oh, honey, I'm so sorry. I never knew it was that terrifying for you."

"You're forgiven" she replied.

I told her we couldn't avoid bridges, and asked her how she would like me to drive over them. She explained that she'd prefer I have both hands on the steering wheel, eyes straight ahead and travel on the inside lane. Since then, I work very hard to drive exactly as she asked. After crossing every bridge she turns to me and says, "Thank you."

How is that healing? In a couple of ways. 1) It's healing for Laura not to be stressed as we travel over bridges. 2) It heals our marriage because it keeps Laura from being annoyed at me!

Forgiveness is Honoring

> *"Be devoted to each other in love. Honor one another above yourselves." –Romans 12:10*

Both repentance and forgiveness are humbling experiences. It is extremely difficult to admit wrong doing, especially in marriage. It is especially hard to forgive when the hurt goes deep.

Don and Diane sat in our office, eyes beet red from crying as they described what had taken place over the last couple years. Don had been given more responsibility—and more pay—at work, but it required him to work many long days. When he came home, he had little or no energy to engage with Diane.

Diane is a recovering alcoholic and attended weekly AA meetings to help maintain her sobriety. While at these meetings she began to converse with another man. Diane described what took place as an emotional affair. This man was giving her the attention she was not receiving from Don.

The reason they were in our office was because Don found the text message between Diane and this man which detailed their plans to take their relationship from emotional to physical.

We met with them for several months and walked them through a book by David Cardar titled *Torn Asunder*. We'd recommend it for any couple who has been through an affair. Those meetings were filled with a lot of angry words from both Don and Diane. However, their tears turned to joy as they rekindled their love for each other.

"Why don't you divorce me? I don't deserve to be forgiven!" Diane asked repeatedly during the process.

Don's answer *every* time was, "I love you, and I want to honor the vows we made."

When we stood at the altar, most every one of us said, "for better or worse." Don chose to honor those words and that vow.

Forgiveness is Holy

> "Father forgive them for they know not what they do."
> —Luke 23:34

So let's not confuse being Holy and being human. We are human, and therefore do human things. For example, Laura has a bad habit of saying, "I'm sorry," for silly things.

"Oh, I've gotten makeup on my blouse. I'm sorry, but I'm going to have to change clothes."

"I'm sorry, but can I get your help with the laundry?"

"I'm sorry, could you pull over at the next exit, I need to use the restroom."

I've finally started saying to her, "Stop apologizing for being human!"

We are human. However, we were made in the image of a Holy God.

"So God created mankind in His own image, in His image He created them; male and female He created them."
—Genesis 1:27

As human beings made in the image of God, we are called to be Holy as He is Holy. We believe this and we practice this, but we are FAR from this most days.

I was talking with a good friend at a dinner party who said he'd been thinking a lot about the passage in Luke mentioned above where Jesus asked forgiveness of the very people who were putting him to death. He said, as a human, he just couldn't wrap his head around the idea of forgiving before the offense is complete. Profound! Jesus is our model of how to be Holy. Forgiveness is a cornerstone.

Honestly, we can't tell you how many times we have had to forgive each other in our three and a half decades of marriage, but that's a good thing. that means no one is keeping score!

Forgiving is not easy. It is hard, at times painful, and for some-one like me, (Laura) it feels like you are excusing the other person's actions. It is important to verbalize the forgiveness so you acknowledge the hurt the other has caused, but it is also important that you internalize the forgiveness. When we take both these steps, the relationship can begin healing. Healing leads to honoring each other. Forgiving becomes a holy act in your marriage.

Your Reflections

Reflect on a time in your marriage when forgiveness paid huge dividends. What difficulties were overcome in order to forgive or be forgiven? Share this with your spouse.

_____

_____

_____

_____

_____

_____

_____

_____

_____

_____

_____

Chapter 12

Restore

The second step in living F-R-E-E is to *restore*. This is the juicy part, and something we love talking about. We believe in a God who restores both lives and marriages, and loves doing it.

If you have heard us speak or read our books, you may have heard that I (Laura) am an HGTV junkie. *Love It or List It* and *House Hunters International* are a couple of my favorite shows. I dream that someday I'll be the one buying a vacation home somewhere in the world.

My newest TV addiction is *Rehab Addict.* The host of the show buys dilapidated old homes in Michigan and Minnesota and restores them to their former grandeur. She goes to a lot of trouble to discover the original design and purpose of each part of the home in order to preserve its original character. It is the coolest thing to watch something dilapidated, broken and abused be completely remade. The restoration of old homes preserves a piece of history that would otherwise be lost.

As I was watching one day, I began to see the parallels in marriage. Marriage is beautiful; sacred. But through time, careless handling, or neglect, our relationships go through crisis and begin breaking down. Maybe you have been taken advantage of, abused, or hurt. You may feel broken and useless. No matter how much damage has been done, God still sees value in your marriage. When he looks at you, he sees the plan he designed you with, and the reasons he brought the two of you together. He desires to take that broken, messy marriage and restore it to the original beauty he designed it for.

Every Marriage Suffers Damage

Everything we encounter on this earth can teach us something about eternity if we are paying attention. God built in so many references to himself in the world around us. He is telling us about himself. We believe, and you may agree, that a healthy, godly marriage between two people may be the closest tangible example on this earth of intimacy, connection and friendship that we are supposed to have with God.

Unfortunately, this side of heaven, it's not a perfect representation. It is still two imperfect humans trying to function as one. That's messy. Some days we get it wrong and hurt each other. Every marriage is going to walk through pain. If we understand that and even expect that, we will be in a better position to heal from it.

The Table

My (Brooke) parents bought an aging farmhouse on the East Coast when I was a toddler. They had, as they put it so frequently, "barely two dimes to rub together." Over the years they fixed it up as they could, but redoing the kitchen was always just out of reach. Now that my dad is close to retirement, they decided to put in the dream kitchen they have always wanted.

A close friend of the family is a builder, and helped my mom design a kitchen for entertaining the family. The pièce de résistance is a beautiful, ten-foot, farm style table made from the sturdy oak beams that supported the original kitchen floor. Mom wanted something that would capture the rustic beauty of an 1800's farmhouse, and this table nailed it. Our first Christmas dinner with all the adult children gathered around that table was the culmination of a dream for my parents.

Not too long after that dinner, I sat my three-year-old down at that same table with a plate of scrambled eggs and a fork. With all the strength her tiny hands could muster, my daughter proceeded to jab her little fork into that oak table and etch two long lines across it's rough-sawn beams. I was livid. I was mortified. What would I tell my mom?

I thought I'd better get ahead of the wrath that was sure to come down on us both. I marched her up to her Nana and demanded that she apologize for what she had just done, which she did. I was trying to think of some way that I could make restitution for the damage done to this irreplaceable piece when my mom said, "Honey, we don't live in a museum."

I will admit, my mom's response surprised me. I might have stood there with my mouth hanging open. This child does not understand what grace she has stumbled upon being the grand-daughter instead of the daughter. If MY three-year-old hands had been the culprit, my hide would have been tanned. How things change from one generation to the next.

Mom's point is totally valid, if unexpected. A table supports the activities in the home that support life. It's a museum quality piece of work, but if it is to be used as it is intended, it's going to get some knicks and dings. We have to be ok with that if we are going to live life to the fullest.

Real life is full of sharp forks that are eventually going to get jabbed into your most precious, tender places by careless hands. It is unavoidable. The alternative is to wall off anything you can't tolerate being damaged and keep it inaccessible. Many of us, as a result of hurt or abuse, try to protect ourselves that way. The problem is, when you close off a part of your heart to keep it safe, you can never go any deeper than that protected place. You will keep people at arms' length, unwilling to get close enough that you could get hurt. All our relationships at that point can only be skin deep. The kind of deep connection we crave with other human beings is only available to us at the risk of some pain.

After the sudden death of a close friend, Alfred Tennyson penned the famous words, "Better to have loved and lost than never to have loved at all." He realized that the human connection we get out of relationships is worth the pain of loss.

Without risk, there can be no intimacy between a husband and wife. But that is the beauty in how God designed marriage! Within the marriage covenant and the commitment it requires, a husband and wife can find safety to make themselves vulnerable and experience a kind of relationship that would otherwise be too risky. Keeping ourselves closed to pain would isolate us from anyone who will truly love us and accept us as we are. Marriage is God's design to create that place of trust we need in order to risk hurt.

If we are willing to fight for one another, marriage itself can provide the protection we need not just to survive, but also to heal from whatever life throws at us. However, even within marriage love is a risk. Our human nature means that none of us will escape unscathed from the battleground of human interaction. Thankfully, we have a God who loves to take what seems irreparably broken and make something beautiful out of it.

The Empty House

Marriages also suffer when they are neglected. This most precious of relationships is something delicate. It requires careful attention to make sure it is in good health. Just like a home, it needs to be kept up with. It's much easier to fix small problems as they arise then to overhaul the entire thing because it wasn't receiving the care it needed every day.

When I was a teenager, a family bought a piece of land adjacent to our farm and built a small house on it. It sat in a big open field at the end of a long driveway. A few years after it was built, the family's small business went under. They declared bankruptcy and the bank took the house.

For a couple years the house sat empty. I grazed my horses on the big field around the house. I watched as it rapidly decayed. The first winter it stood empty, a water line burst and damaged a lot of the interior. Vandals broke in and stole some piping. The front door was damaged, letting the weather and wild animals enter and do further damage. By the time the property sold, the house was unlivable. What was a perfectly functional family home now needed a complete overhaul before it could support life as it was intended.

A neglected marriage is like an empty house. Simple disagreements and minor offenses that could be easily resolved get ignored. Soon more damage is done and before we know it, our marriage can no longer function as the place of safety and refuge God designed it to be. It now needs a complete overhaul to bring it back to what it was. It needs God's restorative power.

God Loves to Restore what is Broken

Do you ever wonder why God allows brokenness in the world? Wouldn't it have been easier for us all if He had just wiped Adam and Eve off the face of the earth and started over with a couple, more obedient humans? It certainly would have saved Him a ton of heartache.

I think part of His decision to allow humanity's ills is that He just loves a good story. God gets to show off, in a way. He shows His might, His power, His creativity. Then it all goes south, and He gets to show us His incredible love, His mercy, His grace. David said that it was His *kindness*, that brings us to repentance. Maybe without the fall and all the restorative work God has done in response to it, we wouldn't have such a beautiful, multi-dimensional picture of who God is.

God is a restorer. He delights in taking what is broken, rejected, hopeless and abandoned and making what only He can make out of it. He knows that His creation, no matter what condition it is in, is worth saving.

The year my husband and I got engaged, we bought our first home. It was a 36-year-old, sixty-foot, single-wide mobile home. We paid cash for it and set it on my parent's farm. We painted it, fixed water-damaged ceilings, put down new carpet, hung curtains and decorated it to our liking. It was nothing fancy, but it was a place a newlywed couple on minimum wage jobs could call their own.

Almost as soon as we moved in, things started breaking. The air conditioner froze up. Pieces of the metal-framed windows fell out. The back door rotted. The washing machine leaked and damaged the floor. We didn't have much money to invest in the home, and neither my husband or I are the handy type to take care of these things ourselves. A lot of things got ignored, covered up or painted over.

Part of the problem was the trailer was old. Very old. It was falling apart faster than our unskilled hands could patch it together. Also, mobile homes aren't built to last. The brand new parts we could buy to fix it weren't much better than the old ones that needed replacing. These homes are built to be economical, lightweight and easy to move from one place to another. They are a sort of temporary solution to an immediate need. Therefore, they don't hold their value. Like cars, they depreciate over time. They reach a point where they are no longer worth the investment to repair, and must be discarded for a newer one. However, not all old things lack value.

If you watch any of the plethora of home repair and design shows on TV these days, you'll know that the craftsman style home is one highly sought after by remodelers and individuals looking for something they can fix up. They are known for a certain quality. They are often filled with lovely materials and unique architectural details hidden just under a century's worth of dust and grime.

We can trace the history of the craftsman home back to nineteenth century Britain. As an industrial revolution took hold, the Arts & Crafts movement responded, rejecting cheaper, mass-produced goods for the quality and character of artisan goods made by hand. As the movement gained ground in America, home designers caught on. They began offering custom home plans for the masses that were small and functional, each with its own unique charm.

Craftsman homes of this era were usually built by their owners, so each one was truly one-of-a-kind. They often included details that are difficult to find or replicate today. Many of these homes are well over 100 years old. Because of the practical design of the home, it's functionality, and the quality of materials used, all these homes need is a little polishing to really shine again, even after 100 years of abuse and neglect.

Your marriage has that same quality of a uniquely designed, hand-crafted masterpiece. It is stamped with the fingerprint of the one who formed it, and there's no other just like yours. It is not replaceable. It is not cheap, easy or disposable. Your marriage is unique, and believe it or not, was blessed by God.

I love what this scripture says about marriage:

> *"He who finds a wife, finds what is good and receives favor from the Lord." -Proverbs 22:18*

If you are married right now, you have something good. It also says you have God's favor on you. Your marriage is blessed. God saw the unique properties of a marriage between you and your spouse before you even met. He knew the impact your lives would have on the world around you. Don't doubt for a second the good that he has planned for you. He has great things in store for your marriage that only you and your spouse can accomplish. That is worth fighting for!

You may feel like you are far off from fulfilling that purpose right now. Let me assure you. God is the Great Restorer and He is rolling up His sleeves, making plans and picking out His tools. He knows exactly what each room of your heart needs to be functional again, and He is so excited about bringing you and your spouse back to life.

Don't Fear the Mess

Restoration is a messy process. If you have ever seen an episode of the TV series *Fixer Upper,* you know Chip Gaines' famous line, "It's demolition day!" He then will proceed to swing a sledge hammer through a wall that must be removed, making a huge mess in the process. Every bit of ruined material has to be removed from the home before the rebuilding process can start. Every project has it's "demolition day."

One of my first mission trips in college was to New Orleans, the spring after Hurricane Katrina hit Louisiana. I'll never forget the scenes of the destroyed homes in the flooded 9th Quarter. I was there nine months after the event, but the homes still sat empty, as if the disaster had happened only yesterday. We were assisting homeowners who had only recently been allowed back in their homes to begin the clean-up process. The houses had been abandoned in the Louisiana heat for three-quarters of a year.

The interior of the home looked like someone had filled it with water, gave it a good shake, then set it back down. Every belonging that the homeowner had lay on the floor. Clothing, documents, furniture, toys, dishes and decorations were piled up to our hips. A black mark on the wall near the ceiling circled the room, marking the highest the water rose on that horrible day. Everything smelled like mold.

Our job was to sort what might be salvageable from what would have to be disposed of. We made little piles of important items and things that may have sentimental value and hauled the rest outside. The salvage pile was very small. The trash pile filled the small yard and spilled out into the street. Once the house was empty of personal belongings, there was still carpet to rip up, moldy sheetrock to be removed, flooring to pry up, damaged cabinets and ruined appliances to haul out. Every item in the home down to the studs in the walls and the beams of the floor had to go. The trash from the inside the ruined homes piled up higher than cars and filled the streets. I have never seen such destruction as I saw walking down those junk-filled streets, looking like the tiny homes had vomited their contents all over them.

Every bit of this exhausting process was absolutely essential. Not a scrap of material that harbored mold could remain in the home. The walls were full of it. The ceiling was full of it. Everything was ruined. It all had to come out, making a huge mess for everyone in the neighborhood to see.

Another clean-up I was involved in was on Staten Island after hurricane Sandy. On a lonely beach road pointing to the river, the waves had broken the dunes during the storm and literally washed homes away. At the end of the street, one three-story home sat in the middle of the road. The older homes a little further from the beach had a lower profile and fared much better. Several homes were undamaged except for the fact that they had been flooded to their roof lines.

The clean up process in those homes was the same as New Orlean's homes that had baked in the sun for months after Katrina. Even though Sandy's cleanup began within days, any wet material in the home would eventually grow the same toxic black mold. So we began stripping the house, first of personal belongings, then demolishing the rest down to the studs and beams.

Any short cuts would have resulted in a toxic environment for those who lived in the home, no matter how clean and beautiful it looked. The messy, ugly, restoration process must begin with cleansing that goes all the way back to the structural elements of the home. It gets way worse before it gets better.

When our marriages are damaged, our automatic response is to cover it up, keep it hidden. We resist dragging our mold-infest junk out into the street for all to see. But whatever we cover up in our hearts continues to fester and spread it's toxin. Soon it gets to the point where it kills life instead of supporting it.

True restoration is going to require a demolition day. Demolition day makes a huge mess, it is ugly, it seems counter-productive at first. However, it is absolutely essential for true healing to take place.

Our World Needs Models of Restoration

There's nothing that has greater power to inspire hope for restoration than to see it done. When you see what is possible, your mind can find it's own path there. I, for example, just plug in "DIY" on pinterest and scroll for a while. Soon I am convinced that I too can change the world with an old pallet and a can of chalk paint.

Many who desperately need hope for their marriages aren't seeking it because they just don't think healing is possible. These may be people you know and rub shoulders with. They feel too far gone, or feel they started off in the wrong place to begin with. God would never want to use a relationship on such poor terms.

Wrong!

Of course that's not true, but they won't believe me. In fact, they may never pick up this book. Only you can change their minds by *showing* them what is possible. The world needs people who, as God heals and transforms their marriages, will live transparently, letting others see what God has done. We are the showcase of His handiwork. When we allow others to see the restoration God has done in us, we spread hope! Suddenly—and perhaps for the first time—the impossible seems possible.

The Restoration Process

Jay with you. There are two requirements for true restoration to happen. The first is to be anger-free. I am going to be honest. This is one I have to work on a lot. I have anger issues. I think most men have anger issues; I don't really know why. I also think most women have jealousy issues—I don't know why. I'm generalizing, here. Some of you don't deal with that. Still, I have to remind myself that the only way restoration is going to happen in my marriage is when I am anger-free.

We also have to be grudge-free. We've got both you and your spouse covered, now. Anger has to deal with... well, anger. Grudges have to deal with jealousy.

Laura here. Sometimes when it comes to forgiveness and restoration, we will hear these words, "I forgive you, but I'll never forget," or, "I'll forgive you, but I'm not going to let you forget." I have said them. I know Jay has said them. Maybe you've said them, too.

Forgiveness doesn't mean the hurt will automatically go away or that you will actually forget. Those memories are always there. You probably *won't* forget. That doesn't mean you cannot *release* the hurt. Forgiveness allows you to release what was done to you and the hurt it caused. It allows you to find freedom—freedom from anger and freedom from holding that grudge. Releasing it through forgiveness allows restoration to happen.

Jay again. Can you remember the first fight you ever had with your spouse? I can. Laura would tell you it was over a couple bucks, but it wasn't. It was over 6 Oreo cookies.

It was 1984, before we got married. Our parents took us to a big gathering in Indianapolis. It was dull and boring. We decided we weren't going to go into the gathering, but we would wait for them at the hotel. This was a big hotel in downtown Indy, before there was a convenience store on every corner. There was, however, a little hotel store where everything is more expensive than it should be.

We were watching TV in the parlor of our suite when Laura said, "Boy, I could really go for something chocolate."

"Cool, what do you want?" I replied.

"I have a craving for Oreos right now." she said. So I headed down to the little store in the hotel lobby and I saw they had a 6-pack of Oreos. I took them to the counter.

"That will be $3.52."

Remember, this was 1984. Minimum wage then was $1.78.

"That's like $0.60 a cookie!" I complained.

The lady just shrugged. Her customers had nowhere else to go, and she knew they would buy the cookies.

Well not me. I went upstairs empty-handed. Laura saw me walk into the room *without* those delicious chocolate Oreos, and we had our first fight. She couldn't believe she wasn't worth the measly $3.52 it would have cost to bring her what she wanted.

Ok, yes. She's worth *far* more than $3.52. That was beside the point.

My mom always told me growing up, to ask this question when you are in the middle of an argument: will whatever you are mad about matter in 100 years? Seriously think about it. I'm driving and someone cuts me off. Will it matter in 100 years? Nope. Someone cuts in front of me in the grocery line. Will it matter in 100 years? Hardly.

My thought was that $3.52, put in a quality mutual fund over 100 years, would matter A LOT. She would have to get over it.

My mom's question points out that we must let go of the sting of the immediate offense if we are to arrive at a place where we are anger-free and grudge-free. We have heard Dr. Gary Chapman talk about this so beautifully. You are going to be angry. You are going to have bitterness. Just don't hold on to it. Don't bring it back up in a day, or in 2 weeks, or in 30 years. Release it and let it go. Then you can get on to the beautiful work of restoring your marriage.

Your Reflections

A bit of self-examination is a good thing. Is there something in your marriage causing you to hold on to anger? Is there an area that you are still holding a grudge? Confess those things to your spouse, and ask God to replace them with His forgiveness and restoration.

_____

_____

_____

_____

_____

_____

_____

_____

_____

_____

_____

Chapter 13

Engage

The third step in living F-R-E-E is to *engage*; engage with your spouse.

I (Brooke) grew up around horses and took riding lessons for many years as a kid. I have spent a good portion of my life riding and training horses, and teaching others to do the same. One term we use quite often in reference to riding a horse is the word "engage."

We use "engage" to describe how a moving horse is using his body. A horse that is engaged will use his hindquarter—the large and powerful hind end of the horse—to push off the ground; to propel himself forward into the movement the rider is asking of him. The engaged horse can easily carry the weight of the rider without damaging his back, he can respond to the rider's cue quickly, and he is able to turn, stop and roll back at a moment's notice. He is easy and pleasant to ride.

A disengaged horse however, is not a pleasure to ride. He leans heavily forward with most of his weight on his front legs, pushing his head and neck toward the ground. He feels heavy under the rider, and has difficulty stopping or turning when the rider asks. Since his back is slack, it is more likely to be sore from the weight of the rider at the end of the ride. He feels like he is being dragged forward, barely able to lift his feet off the ground.

In a word, the disengaged horse is a *lazy* horse, and he is a far cry from the majestic horse galloping across a field in your mind's eye. The engaged horse, however, is a picture of beauty and grace—a perfect reflection of the majesty of his creator.

When you married your spouse, you made a vow to stay engaged through the course of your marriage. It's no problem when you get the better, the richer, or the health part of the deal, but inevitably, life is going to throw some worse, some poorer, and some sickness at you too. When that happens, it's easy to check out or to disengage—to coast in auto-pilot mode and just get through the day, barely lifting your feet off the ground.

Engaging with your spouse is washing his laundry and cooking him a hot meal, even when he hasn't done anything to "deserve" it. It's getting up off the couch to help her with the dishes when your exhausted from a long day at work. It's looking her in the eye when she speaks to you. It's caring about something he loves. Engaging is hard. It takes work. It may require muscles you've never used before. But it is what adds that beauty and grace to your marriage that makes it pleasant even when circumstances are not.

Husbands, Take the Lead

Guys, Jay here. I'm laying the responsibility to engage with our wives on our shoulders. Notice I include myself. We have to take the initiative here, because we were called to pursue our spouses.

Women are wired to want to be desired. Men are wired for the chase. It is God inspired that the man should pursue a woman. That pursuit doesn't end when you finally put a ring on her finger. It is still your honor-bound duty to pursue her, to romance her, and to pleasure her.

Use What You Have

When we were first married, I did a lot of speaking at youth events. I would be gone for the whole weekend. When I would come home from a weekend away, I would always try to bring home a gift. Laura's primary love language is quality time, but her second love language is gifts. She loves to give gifts and she loves to receive gifts.

I was in Toledo, Ohio at an event. I planned to go out on Saturday to buy her a piece of jewelry. I went to a mall jewelry store. I was young. I had no idea how expensive it was going to be. The guy asked what I'm looking for. I replied that I needed something cheap. He shows me a couple things around $100.

I said, "No, you don't understand, I need cheap."

He leads me to another case and shows me something else. $50. Again this is in the 80's and I'm a youth minister. I think I was getting paid $150 for the whole weekend of speaking. Gas alone was going to cost me $50.

"You still don't understand. I need something as nice as you can get, but really *cheap*."

He rolled his eyes and held up a mirror to my face as if to say, "I can show you something cheap!"

I laugh about this now; I know I'm cheap! However, it was my attempt to engage with my wife with what I had. I knew I was coming home after being away for the whole weekend. I knew that even a small gift would mean a lot to her. I was also hoping it was time for some engagement of a different kind.

Choose it When it Doesn't Feel Right

We got invited to be guests on The Big Show with Michael Patrick Shields in Lansing, Michigan. His show is widely listened to in the Great Lakes region.

Very rarely does someone bring up something in a live interview that is unscripted. It's usually mapped out ahead of time what he will ask and what we will say. During this particular interview, however, Michael Patrick made a statement that I will never forget. After listening to us answer one of his questions, he said,

"Jay and Laura, what you're telling me is what we were once compelled to do by infatuation, we must now do by conscious choice."

Wow, Let that sink in. At one point when you fell in love with your spouse, you made every choice to be together, to give grace and to put each other first because you were compelled by infatuation. Unless your still in the honeymoon stage, that infatuation has faded. Now, you have to make a conscious choice to connect. You must choose it even when you don't feel like it.

Consider this quote from American entrepreneur and author, Seth Godin:

"You might be waiting for things to settle down, for the kids to be old enough, for work to calm down, for the economy to recover, for the weather to cooperate, for your bad back to let up just a little. The thing is, people who make a difference never wait for just the right time. They know that it will never arrive. Instead, they make their ruckus when they are short of sleep, out of money, hungry, in the middle of a domestic mess and during a blizzard. Whenever. As long as whenever is now."

Don't wait for things to feel right before you engage with your spouse. Now is the time to pursue your him or her, and a healthy, satisfying marriage. It will never be "the right time."

Maybe you picked up this book during a time when your marriage is going great. You and your spouse are enjoying life. Or maybe you have hit some bumps in the road and you're hoping to recalibrate. Or maybe you are not doing well at all. We get that. We have gone through our own difficult seasons. No matter where you find yourself, now is the time to look at your spouse and commit to re-engaging and seek out how to be the couple God intended you to be.

How Do We Engage?

Engaging with your spouse takes many forms, and will look different for you than it does for us. However, there are two tools we want you to keep in your toolbox to make engagement a little easier. They are meaningful and authentic conversation with your spouse, and meaningful and authentic intimacy with your spouse. In simpler terms, talk and have sex.

Let's take a look at the first part of that: meaningful and authentic conversation. Laura here. When Jay and I have a disagreement, usually one of us shuts down and the other keeps talking. I should have known when Jay decided he was going to have a whole day of insensitivity, that the argument wasn't actually over. He was just shut down. All I get from that point forward is 1-word answers. There's also usually pursed lips involved, too. I know then that I need to give Jay time. He needs silence. I let him recalibrate, and then we can start engaging in meaningful conversation. Sometimes it takes a few hours. It used to take days.

The reason we like to break this down into steps is because you have to forgive your spouse before you can restore the relationship. You have to have restoration before you can engage in meaningful and authentic conversation, and meaningful and authentic intimacy.

Here's what happens in a lot of marriages. Someone offends the other, but they never talk about it. They just try and deal with it on our own. They let it go or try to smooth it over. They don't have a conversation about it. A little later on they might try and have conversation, or might even try to have intimate times, but it can't be meaningful and authentic if you haven't forgiven, restored and engaged. Offense builds on offense, and soon begins to undermine the relationship.

Direct communication plays a huge part in this. You have to say to your spouse, "You hurt my feelings," or, "This is how you made me feel." Verbalizing the problem is part of beginning the forgiveness process.

Once you are communicating honestly again, you can have meaningful and authentic intimacy. What do we mean by meaningful and authentic intimacy? Why, make up sex, of course! Make up sex is some of the best sex. You may have had make up sex since picking up this book. If so, that's wonderful! We're happy to help.

The Shortest Marriage Talk Ever

Jay back with you. Every once in a while I get the privilege of marrying a young couple. I love walking couples through the premarital process because I am helping them lay a foundation for a life-long marriage. I like to take couples pretty deep into the nitty-gritty.

A few weeks before their wedding date, we will start talking about their marriage ceremony and what role they want me to play in it. Nine out of ten couples tell me to "keep it short."

Of course. In other words, they don't want me to preach. That's fine. I then tell them I can give them the shortest marriage talk ever in two sentences.

I will say to the groom, "Young man, for the rest of your life you need to talk more than you think is necessary, because that is what she needs." I then turn to the bride. "And young lady, you need to have sex more than you think is necessary, because that is what he needs. Amen."

They usually ask me to say a little more than that, but it really is that simple.

We know from experience that meaningful and authentic conversation and meaningful and authentic intimacy are both necessary to engage—or re-engage—your spouse.

Your Reflections

How would you rate the level of conversation and intimacy in your marriage? Which of the two do you feel needs more work?

_____

_____

_____

_____

_____

_____

_____

_____

_____

_____

Chapter 14

Experience

The last part of living F-R-E-E is to *experience*. If you are willing to do the hard work of walking through forgiveness, allow God to restore what was broken, and begin to engage meaningfully with your spouse, you can experience a little bit of heaven on earth in your own messy marriage. None of us will achieve perfection this side of heaven, but because of what Jesus has done for us, we can get a taste of all the goodness our marriages were meant to have. I want you to keep three things in your mind as you move forward in healing and growing your marriage.

You are a Mess

I (Jay) had a Sunday School teacher who claimed he never sinned. He was sanctified. For those of you who don't know what it means to be sanctified, in some Christian doctrines there are those who believe in a "second act of grace." Jesus saves us from our sin and then some time later as we mature in Christ we become sanctified or "set apart." Thus we never sin anymore. I don't want to get into a theological discussion, but the day I never sin again is probably going to be the day I see Jesus face to face.

One day I was in a bookstore and saw my Sunday School teacher. He didn't see me. I was most likely in the comic book section. I observed my "sanctified" Sunday School teacher ripping the clerk up one side and down the other. He was using choice words that my parents taught me not to say. Bottom line, he was treating this person in a very hurtful way.

The next time that teacher talked about sanctification, I asked if one could lose their sanctification.

"No," he replied.

"Not even in a bookstore?" I shot back.

The blood rushed out of his face. He just stood there with no reply.

My point is not to shame my old Sunday School teacher. My point is that no matter how good we think we are, we have all fallen short of the mark. You, your spouse, all of us. It's important to remember when we are dealing with each other's shortcomings, that sin is part of the reality we live with on Earth, and there's grace for that.

The Good News

A man died and found himself standing at the pearly gates talking to Saint Peter. Peter said to the man, "It takes 100 points to get into heaven. Tell me what you've done in your life and I'll tell you how many points that gets you."

The man thought about it. "I've been faithful to my wife for our entire married life."

"Great," Peter said, "That gives you one point."

The man thought some more. "I never swore or stole anything."

"That gives you another point."

The man was puzzled. Only one point for each of those? How would he get enough points? "I was involved in my church," he offered, "I served and gave my tithe."

"Wonderful," Peter replied, "Another point."

Now the man was frustrated. "Only three points? I'm never going to get into heaven, except by the grace of God!"

"Ah!" said Peter, "100 Points. Come on in."

It's not about what we do. Nothing we do in our own power can heal a marriage. It is only by God's grace that we can forgive, that brokenness can be restored, that engagement can happen, and that we can experience a piece of heaven. That's good news!

You are in a Messy Marriage

When I (Laura) stood at the altar as a 22-year-old, smitten woman, I believed everything I said in my vows. I meant whole-heartedly when I said that I would stand with my husband "until death do us part." I just didn't realize it would take so long!

It's easy to feel like life will be perfect once you marry your soulmate and get to live happy ever after. It's a different story when the guests have gone home, the honeymoon is over, and now you have to live day in and day out with this person who isn't prince charming all the time.

Rupert Holmes released a song in 1979 entitled "Escape," more affectionately referred to as "The Pina Colada Song." It was the story of a messy relationship where both partners were looking for a way out. The first part of the song goes like this:

I was tired of my lady, we'd been together too long
Like a worn-out recording of a favorite song
So while she lay there sleeping, I read the paper in bed
And in the personals column, there was this letter I read:
"If you like Pina Coladas and getting caught in the rain
If you're not into yoga, if you have half a brain
If you like making love at midnight in the dunes of the cape
I'm the love that you've looked for, write to me, and escape"

Acting on the belief that something new and exciting was what he needed, he writes back:

I didn't think about my lady, I know that sounds kind of mean
But me and my old lady had fallen into the same old d
ull routine
So I wrote to the paper, took out a personal ad
And though I'm nobody's poet, I thought it wasn't half bad:
"Yes, I like Pina Coladas and getting caught in the rain
I'm not much into health food, I am into champagne
I've got to meet you by tomorrow noon and cut through all
this red tape
At a bar called O'Malley's, where we'll plan our escape"

At this point of the song, it sounds like the relationship is over—until the final verse:

So I waited with high hopes, then she walked in the place
I knew her smile in an instant, I knew the curve of her face
*It was my own lovely lady, and she said, **"Oh, it's you"***
*And we laughed for a moment, and I said, **"I never knew,***
That you like Pina Coladas and getting caught in the rain
And the feel of the ocean and the taste of champagne
If you like making love at midnight, in the dunes of the cape
You're the love that I've looked for, come with me, and escape"

Using this song about a planned affair in a book about marriage might seem a little counterintuitive, especially for a person of faith. But, as messy people, we all tend to seek out the "more" that we feel we are missing. As this song so clearly illustrates, the more that we seek can be found right in the messy person you married.

Like the characters in this song, there is so much about your spouse that you haven't discovered yet. Put some effort into seeking and pursuing your spouse, and you will more than likely find what you are looking for.

It Starts Today

Most of us spend so much time feeling guilty about the past or worrying about the future that we fail to live today. Today is all we have. Yesterday is over and there is nothing we can do about that. Tomorrow may never come, as it is not promised to any of us. So, make the most of *today*. Determine that *today* will be the day that you begin to make the most of your messy marriage.

Dress Rehearsal

We are part of a two fold mystery. Christ and his church, and husbands and wives. The thing that makes a mystery so great is that it is mysterious! We can't unravel it all no matter how hard we try, but from time to time we get glimpses.

I believe marriage—when it's good—is like heaven. We've all experienced a time in our marriage where it is good. It tastes good. It feels good. What we've got right is firing on all cylinders. It is beautiful! In that moment, we catch a glimpse of heaven.

It makes me ask this question: what if marriage is just a dress rehearsal for heaven? What if working hard and making sacrifices and taking on the challenges is getting us prepared for an eternity in glory? How would we approach these challenges if we thought like that?

For just a moment, imagine you and your spouse are standing facing one another in the form of a "V". We call that place your little sanctuary. Guard that place and invite Christ to dwell there. Invite him to challenge you, to grow you for the sake of your marriage, but also for the sake of Heaven.

It Made a Difference to One

A man and his young son were walking on an ocean beach in the calm after a tremendous storm. The beach was littered with starfish that had been washed up on shore by the turbulent waves. The son asked his father what would happen to all the starfish. Reluctantly, the father told his son that they would most likely die.

Without hesitation the boy reached down, picked up a Starfish and threw it back into the ocean. The father, in bewilderment, told the son he could not possibly throw all the starfish on the beach back into the ocean. His best efforts would hardly make a difference.

The wise little boy responded, "I made a difference for that one."

Our hope is that in reading this book, you and your spouse may just have been thrown back into the ocean of marriage so that you might thrive.

This is our prayer for each and every one of you:

"Father in heaven, we ask that You would rain down Your Spirit on each couple or individual reading this book. Father, may we live a marriage that is F-R-E-E: may we forgive, restore, engage and experience a little bit of heaven here on earth. May we understand you have brought us together for a reason and for a purpose, and that purpose is to glorify You.

I pray for marriages that are hurting, that they would seek help. Draw them to You. I pray that You would give them the courage to repent, to apologize, to forgive each other, and to re-engage with one another.

Father, for those marriages that are doing well, I praise You and thank You. Let this time they have taken to read this book bear much fruit in their marriage. Lord, we pray that we bring glory to You in Your Kingdom through our lives. In Jesus' precious name. Amen."

Your Reflections

Take a few moments to pray for your marriage and
your spouse.

What is one way that you can start living F-R-E-E today?

_____

_____

_____

_____

_____

_____

_____

_____

_____

_____

Made in the USA
Columbia, SC
11 June 2020

98844029R00109